Introduction to Data Science

"Cracking the Code: Essential Techniques and Tools for Data Science"

Rick Mewis

Table of Contents

Introduction

Background and evolution of data science

The journey of data science, although appearing as a novel innovation of the digital age, possesses a rich tapestry woven over centuries. This progression has been defined by advances in computational technology, refinements in statistical techniques, and a growing reliance of industries on data-driven insights.

Historical Beginnings

The bedrock of what we know as data science can be traced back to the domain of statistics. In the 18th century, thinkers like Sir William Petty brought forward the idea of 'political arithmetic', an early attempt to use data and statistics to address societal challenges. Fast forward to the early 20th century, the concept of statistical quality control began to gain traction, particularly in the industrial sector.

It wasn't until the 1960s that the term "data science" was introduced. However, its essence as a distinct domain started becoming more prominent in the 1980s. This was a period marked by a burgeoning interest in leveraging databases to store information, giving rise to primitive data mining methodologies.

The Rise of Computational Capacities and Storage Solutions

The dawn of the 1990s and 2000s marked a significant turning point. With the advent of the internet and the acceleration of computational abilities, there was a meteoric rise in data generation and collection. Data began to diversify, encompassing not only numbers but also images, text, and even audio.

Alongside, the plummeting costs of data storage meant that vast amounts of data could be stored without breaking the bank. This era underscored the sentiment that data was a reservoir of untapped potential.

The Emergence of Big Data

The sheer volume of data, combined with its rapidly increasing pace and varied forms, gave birth to the 'Big Data' phenomenon. The challenge now pivoted from mere storage to real-time processing and analysis. This led to the development of frameworks such as Hadoop and Spark.

Around this juncture, giants like Google, Facebook, and Amazon started harnessing data to fine-tune their services, marking a paradigm shift towards a data-centric approach in decision-making.

The Confluence of Statistics and Computation

The increased ability to process expansive datasets highlighted a gap – the existing tools and methodologies to interpret this data were becoming inadequate. Thus began a melding of computer science with statistics. This convergence birthed machine learning, offering a suite of algorithms capable of identifying patterns and making data-driven decisions autonomously. Platforms like Scikit-learn in Python, TensorFlow, and subsequently, PyTorch, made these advanced analytical techniques accessible to many.

The Contemporary Landscape of Data Science

By the time the 2010s rolled around, data science had carved out a niche for itself. Its importance was further underscored when the Harvard Business Review hailed it as "The Sexiest Job of the 21st Century" in 2012. The realization dawned that the relevance of data science wasn't exclusive to tech behemoths. Its influence spanned sectors ranging from healthcare and finance to entertainment.

With leaps in artificial intelligence and deep learning, data emerged as the linchpin for technological breakthroughs. Theorized frameworks from the 1950s, like neural networks, suddenly saw a resurgence, resulting in pivotal advances in areas like natural language processing and computer vision.

However, with great power came great responsibility. As data became omnipresent, concerns surrounding its ethical use began to rise. Initiatives like the European Union's General Data Protection Regulation (GDPR) in 2018 highlighted the pressing need to address data privacy concerns.

In Summary

Tracing the path of data science unveils a tale of mankind's unending thirst for knowledge, constantly augmented by the tools of the era. From rudimentary statistical tools to today's intricate neural networks, data science stands as a beacon of the symbiotic relationship between data and innovation. As we navigate the future, it promises to remain a field in flux, influenced by technological strides, societal demands, and moral imperatives.

Importance of data in today's world

In our contemporary setting, data has risen to be considered akin to valuable commodities, drawing parallels with elements like gold. This prominence of data in our daily lives is undeniable as it molds industries, propels tech advancements, and guides decision-making processes. Here's a closer look at the pivotal role data plays in today's intricate tapestry.

Guiding Business Choices and Economic Pathways

In the commercial realm, organizations, regardless of their operational scale, have increasingly turned to insights drawn from data to navigate competitive waters. The era of relying solely on gut instincts or limited datasets to make strategic moves is waning. Modern analytical instruments enable firms to forecast market shifts, decipher consumer habits, streamline operational channels, and refine product strategies. This deep dive into data not only amplifies operational efficacy and revenue streams but also stimulates innovative approaches, allowing businesses to cater more intimately to their customers.

Parallelly, national economies are reaping the rewards of data analytics. Governments are leaning into data to craft informed policies, foresee economic trajectories, and judiciously distribute resources. Through comprehensive data analysis, state authorities can pinpoint developmental gaps, foresee impending obstacles, and introduce effective countermeasures.

Spurring Technological Breakthroughs

Many recent tech marvels, such as deep learning, AI, and cutting-edge robotics, have been fueled by the abundant availability of diverse data. For instance, algorithms in the realm of machine learning rely heavily on expansive datasets for refinement and precision. The leaps we've observed in areas like linguistic AI models or visual recognition algorithms stem from the massive data influx we produce routinely.

Crafting Tailored Digital Journeys

In the virtual world, data acts as a sculptor, carving out unique pathways for users. Digital platforms like Netflix or Apple Music deploy data analytics to curate content recommendations, leading to heightened user engagement. Similarly, e-commerce platforms, exemplified by giants like Amazon, leverage data to curate bespoke shopping experiences, often predicting user desires with remarkable precision.

Elevating Research Horizons

Fields like medicine have witnessed a paradigm shift due to data influx. By pouring over extensive patient records, medical professionals can discern patterns, preempt health crises, and even customize treatments rooted in individual genetic blueprints. In the environmental sector, extensive data aids scientists in modeling ecological shifts and strategizing potential counteractions.

Amplifying Civic Amenities and Security

At the community level, data plays a pivotal role in refining public utilities. Urban centers, now evolving into smart cities, harness data to alleviate traffic congestion, bolster waste management, and guarantee consistent utility services. Security agencies tap into data analytics to highlight potential crime epicenters, thus fortifying public security. Even in the face of calamities, predictive data models have revolutionized relief efforts, ensuring swift responses and resource allocations.

Navigating Ethical Labyrinths

Yet, the omnipresence of data has ushered in intricate ethical mazes, particularly concerning individual privacy. The boon of data-driven personalization comes tethered with the risk of unauthorized intrusions or potential misuse. Consequently, there's a global momentum towards enforcing robust data protection frameworks to ensure personal data sanctity and ethical utilization.

Charting Future Avenues

Poised at the crossroads of the digital epoch, the ramifications of data in sculpting our collective future are profound. The burgeoning domain of the Internet of Things (IoT) is set to unleash data streams at unprecedented magnitudes, further invigorating industries and governance.

Moreover, emerging tech wonders like quantum computing promise to revolutionize data analytics, enabling intricate problem-solving and data dissection in fleeting moments.

To encapsulate, the essence of data in our current era transcends mere volumes. It's our capability to distill, scrutinize, and transform this data into actionable strategies that underscore its significance. As we stride into the future, a calibrated approach, one that harnesses the prowess of data while addressing inherent challenges, will be pivotal.

The objective of the book

Books are more than just tangible entities with pages; they are vessels of wisdom, windows to fresh viewpoints, and instruments of change. Within the expansive terrain of literature, every book is imbued with a distinct aim, be it to inform, enlighten, motivate, or even simply captivate. This particular volume, which you are currently considering, possesses its unique raison d'être, deeply intertwined with the multifaceted domain of data science.

In this era, marked by swift technological strides, data stands out as a transformative force. Often referred to as the 'new gold,' data is the cornerstone of modern industries, economies, and sociocultural frameworks. Its pervasive nature, evident from our daily apps to overarching global decisions, amplifies its relevance. Yet, the true essence of data isn't in its sheer volume but in its insightful interpretation and strategic application.

At its core, this book aspires to unravel the intricacies of data science. Its ambition is to narrow the gap between novices and the vast expanse where data is pivotal. As readers traverse its chapters, they will be guided from the foundational facets of data gathering and cataloging to the more nuanced realms of machine learning frameworks and anticipatory analytics.

Yet, the scope of this volume transcends textbook knowledge. In a context where buzzwords like 'big data' and 'AI' are oftentimes wielded superficially, there's a pressing requirement for deeper discernment. This volume answers that call, offering insight into the broader backdrop of data science, highlighting its developmental trajectory, current utilities, and notably, the ethical challenges it presents.

Data, despite its myriad benefits, ushers in its share of dilemmas. Matters of individual privacy, authorization, and potential exploitation are paramount. Thus, this book adopts a comprehensive stance, exploring the ethical conundrums intrinsic to data science. By juxtaposing technical proficiency with ethical introspection, the book promises a rounded viewpoint, equipping readers not only with data comprehension but also with the acumen to ponder its broader societal repercussions.

Moreover, the dynamic nature of data science, marked by incessant innovations, underscores the need for continual learning. This volume acknowledges this momentum, introducing core concepts and methodologies, thereby priming readers for deeper engagement, and arming them with the foundational acumen to stay attuned to the fluid domain of data science.

A pivotal aspiration of this book is to incite action and foster passion. By shedding light on the nuances of data science and presenting its vast horizon and inherent challenges, it hopes to kindle a fervor within its readers. Whether you're an academic enthusiast, a career professional eyeing data integration, or an inquisitive spirit keen on deciphering the digital undercurrents of our era, this volume is designed to stimulate curiosity, inventiveness, and a spirit of inquiry.

To distill its essence, this book dons multiple hats. It emerges as a beacon of enlightenment, a moral compass, and a springboard for novel ideas. In an age increasingly steered by algorithms and digital pulses, a grasp of data science transitions from being a mere advantage to an imperative. Through its rich amalgamation of technical insights, historical narrative, and ethical introspection, this volume is poised to be your trusted companion on this exhilarating expedition into the data-centric cosmos.

Chapter One

What is Data Science?

Definition and key components

Navigating the intricate corridors of contemporary technology often requires an understanding that goes beyond mere words and into the realm of conceptual depth. Within this vast space, 'definition and key components' are not just terms; they act as guiding beacons, illuminating the foundational facets of this ever-evolving discipline.

Starting with 'definition', one might perceive it as a clear portrayal of a concept's core essence, setting its parameters and differentiating it from related ideas. Within data science and technology, establishing precise definitions is of the essence. As these sectors continually metamorphose, often faster than conventional learning paradigms can capture, it's imperative that all stakeholders, from novices to experts, operate from a shared lexical foundation. This common ground aids in mitigating misconceptions and enhances efficient communication, laying the groundwork for shared understanding and collaboration.

Yet, it's crucial to note that within this space, definitions are not immutable entities. As the technological landscape morphs, so do the meanings and scopes of terms. This dynamic nature of definitions highlights the need for perpetual learning and a willingness to recalibrate one's understanding.

It's less about rote learning and more about grasping evolving fundamentals and adjusting one's perspective accordingly.

Shifting our focus to 'key components', this term dives into the heart of the intricate structures that underpin overarching systems or frameworks. Imagine a sophisticated apparatus – its efficacy is determined not merely by its external appearance but by the harmonious interplay of its internal parts. Analogously, in areas like data science, delving into key components is akin to unearthing the foundational mechanics of complex systems.

Take, for instance, a machine learning model. At its essence, it might be perceived as a digital entity that refines its task efficacy based on accrued experience. However, this broad interpretation gains tangible depth only when dissected into its key constituents: the sourced data, computational procedures, distinct phases of training and testing, and iterative feedback mechanisms, among others.

Each of these components, with its distinct role and function, collaborates to orchestrate a cohesive entity. And, akin to the fluid nature of definitions, these components too are not set in stone. Emerging research and innovative methodologies can redefine these elements, transforming their relevance or even rendering them obsolete.

Yet, the merit of understanding these core components transcends academic or vocational objectives. It forms the bedrock upon which additional insights and innovations can be layered. A holistic grasp of these fundamental elements empowers professionals to explore, innovate, and enhance, propelling the discipline to newer horizons.

To encapsulate, 'definition and key components', while ostensibly simple terms, wield significant weight within the spheres of data science and technology. They offer a structured lens through which the intricate tapestry of technological progress can be viewed and understood. Grasping these foundational concepts is not merely advantageous; it's a prerequisite for anyone aspiring to delve deep into the intricate nuances of this vibrant field. As with any sturdy structure, the foundation is paramount. In the context of data science and technology, the definitions and key components provide that crucial foundational stability.

Overview of data science processes

Data science is frequently recognized as the fulcrum of contemporary tech innovations. At its core, it's a systematic domain, governed by distinct stages that mold unrefined data into meaningful interpretations. This synopsis endeavors to shed light on the primary steps intrinsic to these stages, offering a comprehensive view into the sophisticated interplay of methodologies, instruments, and strategies that define data science.

Data Acquisition: The commencement of any data science journey hinges on procuring data. This entails gathering data from an array of sources, including databases, online services, connected devices, or manual inputs. In our expansive digital age, the sheer magnitude of accessible data is overwhelming. Nevertheless, the real task lies in pinpointing data sets that resonate with the objective in focus.

Data Cleaning: Post-data collection, the data is seldom in an impeccable state. Inconsistencies, duplications, and errors often pepper the datasets. Thus, data cleaning, sometimes termed data preprocessing, emerges as a vital step to sift through this data, excising superfluous elements and rectifying voids. An array of methods, such as standardization, transformation, and outlier management, are enlisted to ensure data credibility and analysis readiness.

Data Exploration: Armed with a streamlined dataset, the ensuing phase is exploratory data analysis (EDA). This pivotal process unveils inherent patterns, correlations, and irregularities in the data. Diverse tools, ranging from visual aids to rudimentary modeling approaches, are employed during EDA, facilitating a preliminary comprehension that steers subsequent intricate analyses.

Feature Engineering: Recognizing the salience of specific data attributes is essential for crafting a potent model. The practice of feature engineering entails pinpointing, reshaping, or even crafting pivotal attributes for a designated model. This phase can profoundly amplify a model's predictive accuracy by focusing on salient data facets.

Modeling: At this stage, the essence of data science takes center stage: devising descriptive or predictive models. The nature of the problem—classification, regression, grouping, or suggestion—dictates the choice of algorithms. Possible methods span from rudimentary tools like linear regression to sophisticated approaches like neural networks. A pivotal aspect here is data bifurcation into training and validation subsets to validate the model's performance and guard against over-generalization.

Model Evaluation: Post-training, the efficacy of a model is put to the test. Evaluating the model entails harnessing specific benchmarks and techniques to assess metrics like accuracy, sensitivity, specificity, or other relevant performance indicators. This evaluation elucidates both the model's competencies and its constraints.

Deployment: The true mettle of a model is tested upon its integration into operational environments. This transition facilitates the model's application for real-time or periodic processing of fresh data. Essential considerations at this juncture encompass system scalability, response times, and overall resilience.

Monitoring and Maintenance: Given the data's evolving nature, it's imperative to understand that deployed models cannot remain stagnant. Shifting trends, consumer behaviors, and myriad external elements can influence model relevance. Vigilant monitoring becomes indispensable to identify such deviations. Periodic model updates or enhancements ensure its alignment with the latest data trends.

To encapsulate, data science is characterized by its cyclical essence. Insights derived from advanced phases often circle back, enriching initial phases and ushering in refinements. Additionally, the dynamic fabric of data science is ceaselessly evolving, punctuated by the advent of novel techniques and tools. Staying updated, while firmly grounded in core processes, remains paramount for efficacious data science undertakings.

The trajectory from rudimentary data to profound revelations is multifaceted and nuanced. It necessitates a harmonious melding of analytical insight, tech prowess, and industry-specific acumen. Nevertheless, it's this intricate choreography of processes that bestows data science with its unparalleled capacity, empowering entities and individuals to unlock data's dormant potential.

Data science vs. other fields

In the modern era marked by digital transformation, data science has risen as a pivotal discipline. Celebrated for its capacity to catalyze change, it fuses statistical approaches, intricate computational methods, and sector-specific knowledge to distill valuable revelations from intricate datasets. To better appreciate its contours, it's instructive to contrast data science with its peer disciplines, discerning both its convergences and disparities.

Statistics: The shared space between data science and statistics is evident. Both arenas harness quantitative data to inform conclusions. Yet, while statistics delves deeply into data distribution, hypothesis verification, and probabilistic models, data science seamlessly integrates these elements with progressive computational processes and predictive paradigms. Notably, data science often grapples with the challenges and opportunities of 'Big Data', placing an emphasis on forward-looking insights.

Computer Science: The synergy between data science and computer science is palpable. Foundational algorithms, computational methods, and data management strategies that underpin data science have their genesis in computer science. However, they diverge in purpose. Computer science spans a vast expanse, from software crafting to systems architecture, whereas data science zeroes in on gleaning insights from typically voluminous and multifaceted datasets.

Machine Learning: Perceived as a branch of data science, machine learning (ML) concentrates on sculpting algorithms enabling machines to discern patterns and decide based on data, sidestepping explicit coding. While data science incorporates ML strategies, it also navigates other terrains like data curating, analytical methodologies, and strategies beyond just algorithm-based interpretations.

Business Intelligence (BI): BI is anchored in scrutinizing historical and current data to steer business strategies. It leverages visualization, dashboarding, and historical analyses. Conversely, data science often peers into the horizon, utilizing predictive and prescriptive analytics to project future trajectories and recommend optimal pathways. Its purview extends beyond BI's primarily retrospective lens.

Data Analytics: Though occasionally conflated, data analytics and data science are distinct. Data analytics typically processes and statistically dissects extant datasets to discern patterns and insights. In contrast, data science embraces a more expansive mandate, including intricate algorithm crafting, machine learning, and forward-looking modeling to address intricate data challenges.

Information Technology (IT): IT encompasses the development, upkeep, and deployment of software, networks, and computer systems for data handling and dissemination. While data science thrives on the platforms and tools established by IT, its primary quest is the sophisticated analysis and interpretation of said data.

Operational Research: Grounded in harnessing mathematical frameworks and analytical techniques for decision-making, operational research often operates within structured models. Data science, meanwhile, encounters a more fluid landscape, dealing with diverse and extensive data sets, melding both fixed and chance-based models.

While making these delineations, it's vital to recognize that these nuances aren't about elevating one field over another. They emphasize the distinct facets and priorities of each domain. Moreover, data science's real vigor often emerges when it's interwoven with the insights and methods of these other domains.

In summation, data science, equipped with a diverse arsenal, resides at the crossroads of several disciplines, absorbing and augmenting multiple fields. Its malleable and collaborative essence not only cements its contemporary relevance but also underscores its potential to spearhead advancements in the data-centric world we inhabit.

Chapter Two

Data Collection and Cleaning

Sources of data

In today's data-centric world, data stands as the linchpin for numerous analytical and interpretative activities. The success of data-driven initiatives greatly depends on the caliber, pertinence, and breadth of the foundational data. As we navigate the digital age, data emanates from an astonishing variety of sources. Grasping the extent and potentialities of these data origins necessitates a holistic examination of their diverse and expansive nature.

Transactional Data: A predominant form of data, transactional data, is captured during routine business activities. Whether it's a consumer purchasing an item, banking activities, or other commercial interactions, every event engraves a distinct data imprint. This category is essential for gleaning insights into customer inclinations, market trends, and business performance.

Log Files: Produced by systems, applications, and networks, log files offer a meticulous chronicle of events and operations. From a web server recording user interactions to an application log capturing anomalies, these records are crucial for diagnostic, security, and analytical purposes.

Social Media Platforms: Modern digital platforms, spanning from Facebook to Snapchat and Pinterest, churn out vast amounts of data continually. Every user-generated content, interaction, and even passive action is a fountain of rich, typically unstructured, data. This abundance of information provides a window into societal moods, emerging patterns, and user predilections.

Sensors and IoT Instruments: The ascendancy of the Internet of Things (IoT) has catalyzed a surge in data creation. Devices, such as wearable gadgets, industrial detectors, and interconnected household appliances, incessantly produce data. This continuous stream, often captured in real-time, is pivotal for applications like health monitoring, predictive diagnostics, and more.

Public Data Repositories: Many institutions, from government bodies to academic entities, periodically make datasets accessible to the public. These encompass demographic details, economic metrics, health data, and a plethora of other categories. These meticulously curated datasets are foundational for a spectrum of analytical and research initiatives.

Surveys and Feedback Forms: Purpose-driven data collection methods, like surveys or feedback tools, remain a cornerstone for obtaining specific data. Administered either digitally or traditionally, these instruments fetch insights into individual preferences, experiences, and viewpoints.

Visual Data: Advancements in technologies deciphering images and videos have elevated multimedia as a critical data reservoir. Domains such as medical diagnostics, pattern identification, and facial detection hinge on this visual information.

Sound Data: Progress in audio analytics and voice processing has spotlighted audio data in various applications. From digital voice assistants to the examination of customer interactions over calls, audio data is a repository of sentiment and content.

Geographical Data: Sourced from satellites, geolocation tools, and meteorological stations, geographical data offers location-centric insights. Its significance is palpable in fields like environmental research, transportation planning, and agriculture.

Genetic Data: Within the spheres of medical science and biotechnology, the unraveling of human genetic sequences offers a wealth of intricate data. This data is instrumental in deciphering genetic patterns, identifying predispositions, and advancing therapeutic research.

In summing up this exploration of data origins, it becomes apparent how pervasive and multifaceted data is in contemporary society. Recognizing the unique attributes and applications of each source reinforces the importance of competent management, thorough analysis, and discerning interpretation. As industries and societies evolve, our adeptness in channeling these profuse data sources will profoundly influence future directions. Consequently, understanding and leveraging these diverse data origins is not just a technical challenge but a strategic necessity.

Techniques for collecting data

Data's pivotal role in analytical undertakings emphasizes the significance of its acquisition phase. This initial collection is a linchpin for subsequent examinations and interpretations. Consequently, ensuring accuracy and relevance during this phase is essential. Over the ages, various methodologies have been developed and refined to streamline this vital process, each tailored to cater to specific data types and analytical goals.

Surveys: A stalwart in the data collection realm, surveys offer a direct approach to gathering structured information. Deployed online, via calls, or in-person, surveys cater to a vast range of subjects, delivering both numeric and descriptive insights. Crafting unbiased, lucid questions and targeting a diverse participant pool is essential for reliable outcomes.

Observational Techniques: This passive approach entails systematically observing and noting behaviors or occurrences in their natural environment. Predominantly used in areas such as behavioral studies or consumer research, observations provide genuine glimpses into real-world actions and reactions.

Experiments: Grounded in rigorous scientific principles, experiments are structured to validate or refute hypotheses in a controlled setup. By adjusting specific parameters and tracking the results, experimental methodologies can deduce direct cause-and-effect relationships, making them crucial in various disciplines.

Interviews: Characterized by depth, interviews are organized discussions tailored to extract detailed insights on particular topics. Although they require more effort than surveys, the depth and granularity of information retrieved are unparalleled, especially for comprehensive studies or expert consultations.

Focus Group Discussions: Blending elements of interviews and surveys, focus groups foster collaborative dialogues among a pre-selected cohort. Orchestrated by a facilitator, these conversations unravel group sentiments, perceptions, and viewpoints on designated topics.

Digital Analytics Tools: In the online space, user interactivity with platforms, apps, or websites generates a consistent data flow. Instruments like Google Analytics or similar platforms systematically accumulate this data, shedding light on user tendencies, preferences, and engagement metrics.

Sensors and Mechanized Gathering: The surge of the Internet of Things (IoT) and integrated sensors across devices, from smartphones to industrial equipment, has championed automated data recording. Applications range from real-time surveillance, and locational data acquisition, to capturing environmental parameters.

Web Data Extraction: A vast reservoir of information on the internet, although publicly visible, isn't always directly downloadable. Tools designed to mine this data transform web content into organized datasets. This powerful method, however, requires a mindful approach to respect ethical boundaries and web usage terms.

Documentary Research: Tapping into pre-existing data records or documents is often termed archival or secondary research. By delving into historical archives, earlier surveys, or official data repositories, this approach provides a historical context and aids trend evaluations.

Ethnographic Investigation: Stemming from anthropological roots, ethnographic methodologies emphasize in-depth, prolonged observations. By integrating within specific groups or communities, researchers aim to decode underlying customs, behaviors, and societal dynamics from an ingrained perspective.

Feedback Channels: Online services and businesses routinely incorporate feedback systems, from user ratings to comments, to assimilate user feedback and critiques. This ongoing influx acts as a real-time gauge of user contentment and potential enhancement areas.

A resonating aspect of data collection is the equilibrium between scope and granularity. Some methodologies, like surveys, cover expansive data over large cohorts, while others, such as interviews, focus on minute details. Integral to these methods are the ethical standards encompassing informed consent and data confidentiality, highlighting the essence of a principled approach.

In summation, the rich tapestry of data collection methodologies presents an arsenal for data aficionados. The strategic selection of the appropriate method, or a blend thereof, aligned with the research intent and backdrop, ensures that the analytical journey is initiated on solid ground, priming the path for impactful discoveries and judicious conclusions.

Importance and methods of cleaning data

The vast domain of data science showcases a crucial yet frequently undervalued step: the purification of datasets, more commonly known as data cleaning. While high-profile data analytics techniques often capture the limelight, the groundwork established by thorough data cleaning can be the determining factor in the accuracy and utility of the subsequent analysis. Clean data is pivotal, as even state-of-the-art algorithms can produce misguided outcomes if based on disorganized or erroneous information. Let's examine the salience of this preparatory step and the strategies employed to achieve data integrity.

The indispensable role of data cleaning stems from challenges inherent to the acquisition and maintenance of datasets. Data from diverse origins, unintentional human lapses, system discrepancies, or evolving data configurations can lead to misalignments, redundancies, or deviations. Overlooking these inconsistencies can misguide analytical interpretations, compromise predictive capabilities, and lead to erroneous conclusions.

Addressing Absent Data: A widespread concern in many datasets is the presence of absent or undefined entries. These absences can be attributed to various circumstances, such as overlooked data points, device glitches, or intentional survey non-responses. Depending on the dataset context and the degree of missing information, several strategies can be deployed:

27

Data Estimation: This method predicts absent values based on other relevant data. Common techniques include using the mean, median, or mode for simple replacements. Advanced strategies, like regression models or machine learning methods like k-Nearest Neighbors, can offer a nuanced estimation.

Entry Removal: When the absent data appears random and isn't substantial, straightforward removal of such instances might be the most pragmatic approach.

Resolving Data Deviations: Outliers or data aberrations can sway statistical results and model evaluations. It's crucial to distinguish genuine extreme values from mistakes.

Graphical Tools: Utilizing plots such as scatter diagrams, box plots, or frequency distributions can visually pinpoint potential outliers.

Numerical Techniques: Approaches like the Z-score or the IQR (Interquartile Range) can algorithmically detect and manage outliers.

Uniform Scaling: Data attributes with different magnitudes can mislead some distance or gradient-based algorithms. Bringing features to a uniform scale is vital.

Range Scaling: This technique adjusts features to fall between specified values, typically between 0 and 1.

Standard Score Scaling: This method transforms features to achieve a zero mean and a unit variance.

Duplicate Resolution: Repeated records can bloat datasets and skew analysis. Processes that pinpoint and discard these repetitions uphold data accuracy and efficiency.

Ensuring Data Integrity: It's fundamental to guarantee that data aligns with predefined patterns or standards. As an example, ensuring consistent patterns in phone numbers or verifying the correctness of email formats can forestall potential downstream pitfalls.

Data Refinement: Occasionally, original data might not be optimally structured for analysis. Refinements such as log transformations, categorizing numeric data, or translating categorical variables into numeric representations prime the data for further steps.

Harmonizing Data Labels: This is especially pivotal for categorical data, ensuring that different categories are labeled uniformly. For instance, making certain that designations like "U.S.A.", "USA", and "United States" are consistently applied.

Optimizing Attributes: Beyond mere cleaning, enriching a dataset might involve generating new attributes from current ones. This can highlight latent trends or connections, augmenting the dataset's analytic potential.

Navigating the intricacies of data cleaning might seem daunting. Yet, with the assistance of tools—ranging from programming frameworks like Python's Pandas to specialized applications such as Talend or DataWrangler—the journey becomes methodical and productive. Crucially, data cleaning isn't a universal process; the tactics chosen must resonate with the dataset's characteristics and the overarching analytical aims.

To wrap up, as the world leans more into data-centric decision-making, the quality and trustworthiness of the foundational data become pivotal. Though the process of data cleaning is exacting and may require multiple iterations, it guarantees that the analytic bedrock is steadfast. The essence lies not just in amassing voluminous data but in ensuring its pristine quality.

Chapter Three

Exploratory Data Analysis (EDA)

Why EDA is crucial

Within the intricate matrix of data analytics, Exploratory Data Analysis (EDA) operates as an essential precursor, shaping the trajectory of subsequent investigative endeavors. Despite the emphasis frequently placed on advanced analytics and complex modeling in the realm of data science, the groundwork laid by EDA is unequivocally vital. This preliminary examination is more than just a superficial overview; it's a comprehensive investigation into data's nuances, highlighting patterns, pinpointing irregularities, and fostering the foundation for hypothesis formulation and deeper analysis. Let's delve into the profound relevance of EDA in the data analysis lifecycle.

Deciphering Data Patterns: Datasets, at first glance, might appear enigmatic. EDA, equipped with various visual tools and descriptive statistics, decodes this complexity. It unravels the intricate weave of variables, revealing correlations and providing a cogent perspective of the data's landscape. Such insights guarantee that further analyses stand on a platform of genuine comprehension, not mere conjecture.

Spotting Irregularities: Authentic, real-world data isn't always immaculate. Inconsistencies, aberrations, and gaps are commonly encountered. EDA illuminates these discrepancies. Techniques like scatter plots or box diagrams accentuate data aberrations, allowing for early detection and rectification. This proactive approach ensures that subsequent stages of analysis remain uncompromised.

Guiding Analytical Approaches: The effectiveness of machine learning models hinges on their alignment with the nature of the data. Data with discernible linear relationships might be aptly tackled by linear models, while intricate patterns could require more elaborate techniques. EDA, by revealing these nuances, acts as a beacon in the selection of suitable analytic methods.

The catalyst for Feature Refinement: Insights from EDA can often serve as the genesis for feature engineering—transforming or introducing variables to accentuate inherent patterns. Recognizing correlations or inherent clusters in the data during EDA can suggest the creation of new variables, enhancing model performance.

Checking Analytic Preconditions: Several algorithms and statistical methods operate based on specific preconditions—like data normality or the independence of variables. Through EDA, these foundational requisites are meticulously vetted, safeguarding the integrity and reliability of future analyses.

Facilitating Stakeholder Engagement: Beyond its technical merits, EDA's visual outcomes—be it trend visualizations or correlation matrices—translate complex data stories into digestible formats. For those not deeply entrenched in data analytics, EDA's graphical representations provide clear, relatable insights, bridging the gap between data professionals and organizational decision-makers.

Risk Abatement: Venturing into intricate analyses without initial exploration is fraught with challenges. Misinterpretations or oversight can skew results. EDA, by granting a comprehensive understanding of the data landscape, minimizes such hazards, ensuring that subsequent analyses are both on-point and valuable.

Optimizing Resource Utilization: Resource-intensive models can strain both time and infrastructural resources. With EDA's clear insights into data attributes, there are instances when simpler techniques might be equally effective, or specific data subsets emerge as pivotal. Such discernment leads to efficient resource deployment and cost-effective outcomes.

To distill the essence, EDA is akin to the groundwork in strategy formulation—it elucidates the environment, highlights challenges, and showcases potential avenues. While the attraction of sophisticated algorithms and models is robust, the detailed, foundational exploration offered by EDA is the anchor that ensures their efficacy. This analytical phase merges methodical evaluation with intuitive understanding, juxtaposing the tangible with the abstract.

In summation, as data solidifies its role as the cornerstone of contemporary enterprises and innovations, the methodologies we employ for its interpretation gain heightened significance. EDA, melding visualization techniques with statistical scrutiny, emerges as the sentinel, ensuring our data-centric endeavors are grounded in depth and insight.

Descriptive statistics

The discipline of descriptive statistics is fundamental to the realm of data interpretation, offering tools to efficiently summarize and describe vast datasets. This analytical approach not only simplifies data representation but also paves the way for deeper inferential statistical explorations by initially streamlining the data landscape. A closer look at descriptive statistics elucidates its pivotal role in shaping data-centric insights.

Central to descriptive statistics is its ability to distill data's primary characteristics through numbers and illustrative techniques. Instead of navigating through dense, raw data, these statistics present an organized and clearer perspective, emphasizing data tendencies, patterns, and variances.

Central Tendency: Measures of central tendency are foundational, providing insights into the dataset's core. The most utilized measures encompass:

Mean (Arithmetic Average): It represents the sum of all data points divided by the total count. While providing an immediate insight, its value can be influenced by extreme data points.

Median: This is the central value when a dataset is organized in order. For even datasets, it's the average of the two centermost figures. It offers a stable measure, especially when distributions are skewed.

Mode: It showcases the most recurrent value within a dataset. Data can exhibit one mode (unimodal), two modes (bimodal), or multiple modes (multimodal).

Spread or Dispersion: Delving into the spread of data reveals its variability. Key indicators include:

Range: The difference between the dataset's highest and lowest figures. Though straightforward, it's highly influenced by outliers.

Variance: Calculates the average of squared deviations from the mean. Its squared units can make it a bit intricate for direct interpretations.

Standard Deviation: Representing the variance's square root, gives the typical deviation of data points from the mean. Its utility in assessing data variance is widely acknowledged.

Quartiles and Interquartile Range (IQR): Quartiles segment the data into four equal portions. The IQR, spanning between the first and third quartiles, signifies the spread of the central 50% data, providing resistance against outliers.

Shape of Distribution: The distribution's contour is also described through descriptive statistics.

Skewness: Denotes distribution's asymmetry. A rightward lean indicates a positive skew, while a leftward tilt signals a negative skew, offering insights into the distribution's balance.

Kurtosis: Reflects the distribution's tail extremities. Elevated kurtosis indicates pronounced deviations, suggesting outliers or thick tails.

Complementing these numeric metrics are visual tools like histograms, which delineate data distributions, and box plots, which pictorially present data spread and outliers.

However, the practical implementation of descriptive statistics goes beyond mere calculations. Especially with vast data reservoirs, understanding data subtleties becomes paramount. It's not just about deriving a series of figures; it's about decoding the narrative they portray.

Furthermore, in research realms, descriptive statistics often form the backdrop for subsequent inferential studies. By crystallizing the data overview, these statistics steer researchers toward framing hypotheses and choosing relevant statistical evaluations.

In the commercial sector, the capabilities of descriptive statistics transform extensive operational or transactional datasets into actionable knowledge. For instance, by encapsulating sales figures, businesses can pinpoint trends or deviations, underpinning strategic moves.

In summation, descriptive statistics emerge as a foundational pillar in data analytics. By reformatting and clarifying raw data, it acts as the intermediary between raw observations and profound insights, setting the stage upon which further data models or statistical methods can be deployed. In today's data-abundant age, mastering the nuances of descriptive statistics is indispensable, cementing its role as a facilitator of informed analytical endeavors.

Visualization techniques

The art of deciphering data finds its most eloquent expression in visualization techniques. Through these techniques, vast and often intricate numerical sets are elegantly metamorphosed into relatable, straightforward visuals. This transformative process is instrumental, in ensuring that multifaceted data becomes accessible and illuminating to a wide audience.

1. Bar and Column Diagrams: A staple in the visualization toolkit, these diagrams are optimal for contrasting subsets of data. Horizontal representations are seen in bar charts, while their vertical counterparts are termed column charts. Their strength lies in elucidating data differences across distinct categories.

2. Line Charts: Perfect for tracking evolution over durations, line charts provide a visual narrative of trends. Whether monitoring financial market movements or assessing periodic sales metrics, the unbroken lines in these charts capture the essence of data's progression.

3. Circular Graphs: Commonly known as pie charts, these are invaluable when presenting componential data. Their strength lies in portraying categorical data and its relation to a collective sum.

4. Point Distribution Graphs: Better known as scatter plots, they display data entities within a bi-dimensional framework. They shine a light on how two variables might interact, hinting at correlation or potential influencing factors.

5. Data Distribution Graphs: More than mere bar diagrams, histograms outline how continuous data is spread out. By segmenting data into defined slots, they reveal the density of data points within each slot, presenting an overview of where data aggregates.

6. Box and Whisker Diagrams: Deployed to represent data spread, they capture data distribution through five key data points: minimum, first quartile, median, third quartile, and maximum. Their design is adept at highlighting data range and potential outliers.

7. Intensity Maps: Known to many as heatmaps, they utilize shades to denote data values within a grid. Commonly employed to pinpoint density or intensity, they're seen in online user analytics or matrix correlation depictions.

8. Nested Diagrams: Treemaps, as they're called, portray data within a hierarchical structure using encapsulated rectangles. Each sub-segment is distinguished by size or hue, portraying a condensed and data-rich visual.

9. Geographic Data Maps: By overlaying data on geographical outlines, these visualizations offer a spatial perspective. Ideal for regional sales analysis, epidemiological studies, or demographic breakdowns, they provide insights anchored in geography.

10. Interlinking Diagrams: For data sets where interconnectedness is central, network diagrams come into play. From social media analysis to infrastructure outlines, they spotlight the ties between different nodes.

Today, advanced digital solutions, including software such as Power BI, and Tableau, and libraries in Python like Seaborn or Matplotlib, have broadened access to sophisticated visualization creation. Yet, it's vital to remember that effective visualization isn't just about aesthetics. It's essential to match the technique to the message and the data's nature. For instance, while circular graphs excellently depict market distribution, they might be less adept at chronicling a stock's decade-long journey.

Moreover, in this era of data democratization, upholding ethical standards in visualization has never been more crucial. Misrepresentations, whether through skewed axes or deceptive color palettes, can compromise data integrity and misguide decisions.

In summation, visualization techniques are more than mere tools; they're the storytellers of the data-driven era. As data continues its exponential growth, these techniques become our compass, guiding us through vast data oceans and revealing their hidden treasures.

Chapter Four

Fundamentals of Statistics in Data Science

Basic statistical terms and concepts

Statistics, a pivotal branch of mathematics, equips us with tools essential for data assessment, analysis, and interpretation. Central to its vast landscape are elementary concepts and terminologies that lay the groundwork for more intricate methodologies. An understanding of these rudimentary terms is indispensable for anyone venturing into empirical research, decision-making based on data, or analytical examinations.

1. Population vs. Sample:

Population: Encompasses the full set of subjects or entities of interest. In a study context, it might mean every individual in a nation, all units of a product, or each transaction in a database.

Sample: A chosen subset of the population that's subjected to analysis. Proper sampling ensures this subset adequately represents the larger population, facilitating insightful extrapolations about the entire population.

2. Data Variables:

Data attributes that can be quantified or categorized include:

Continuous: Variables with values that span a continuum, e.g., age or temperature.

Discrete: Variables with distinct, countable values like the number of cars in a garage.

Categorical: Variables that fit into distinct categories but aren't inherently numerical, such as nationalities or types of fruits.

3. Core Measures of Central Tendency:

These metrics provide a snapshot of a dataset's "central" point.

Mean: The cumulative sum of all data points, divided by their number.

Median: The central value when data is arranged in sequence. With even data counts, it's the average of the two central figures.

Mode: Represents the most recurrent value in a dataset.

4. Dispersion Metrics:

Indicators of variability or spread in data.

Range: The gap between the highest and lowest values.

Variance: Shows how each data point deviates from the mean, squared to ensure positivity.

Standard Deviation: The square root of the variance, signifying the data's deviation from its average.

5. Probability:

It gauges the chance of an event's occurrence, with values from 0 (absolute impossibility) to 1 (certainty).

6. Hypothesis Assessment:

This method evaluates assertions about specific parameters. It starts with a baseline (null hypothesis) against an alternative. The statistical tests gauge the probability of observing certain data under the assumption that the null hypothesis holds.

7. P-value:

In hypothesis assessment, the p-value measures the odds of getting results as, or more, extreme than those observed, assuming the null hypothesis is true. Lower p-values often lead to discarding the null in favor of the alternative.

8. Confidence Intervals:

An interval estimate of a population parameter. For instance, a 95% confidence interval implies that 95 times out of a hundred, the interval would enclose the true parameter.

9. Understanding Correlation vs. Causation:

Correlation: Shows the linear relationship intensity between two entities, with values between -1 and 1.

Causation: Indicates that one variable's alteration directly impacts another. It's vital to discern that correlation doesn't necessarily denote causation.

10. Bias and Data Variation:

Bias: Indicates persistent discrepancies in measurements or deductions.

Variability: Demonstrates the degree of difference among data points.

11. The Gaussian Curve:

Also known as the normal distribution, it symbolizes a curve where data is symmetrically distributed, with the majority of data points huddled near the mean.

12. Regression Analysis:

A method to ascertain the character and strength of relationships between a dependent variable and its predictors.

13. Data Outliers:

These are anomalous data points that significantly diverge from the rest. Their origin might be genuine anomalies or errors, and they can notably influence standard deviation and mean.

14. Quartiles and Data Percentiles:

Quartiles: They segment a dataset when arranged in order, into four equal segments.

Percentiles: They partition a dataset into 100 equal parts.

To encapsulate, these elementary statistical principles form the cornerstone for data comprehension. They empower users to spot meaningful trends, forecast outcomes, and craft compelling narratives from data that might otherwise seem disconnected. In the present era, replete with data and advanced analytics, this "grammar of data" is undeniably indispensable, guiding us to coherent narratives, discernable patterns, and judicious choices.

Probability distributions

In the vast realm of statistics, probability distributions serve as a cornerstone, offering an elegant means to represent potential outcomes and their corresponding probabilities. They craft a systematic structure for depicting events quantitatively, underpinning predictive modeling, risk evaluation, and in-depth analysis. To navigate through the extensive domain of probability distributions, it's imperative to distinguish between the discrete and continuous categories and appreciate their significance.

Discrete Distributions:

Discrete variants of probability distributions concern events that take place in clear, separate intervals. Classic cases include outcomes of a dice throw or a coin flip.

Binomial Distribution: Envision an activity that yields only two possible outcomes, typically classified as "success" and "failure". If this activity is iterated multiple times, the pattern of "successes" over these iterations can be described by the binomial distribution. Fundamental parameters are the total number of attempts, represented by n, and the probability of witnessing success in a single attempt, represented by p.

Poisson Distribution: This formulation is useful when estimating how often an event might occur within a specified timeframe or region. It's ideally suited for scenarios where events manifest at a recognized constant rate and are spaced out independently of preceding occurrences. It can model events such as the number of incoming emails within an hour or call frequencies in a helpline center.

Geometric Distribution: This distribution calculates the trials required before observing the first success. If an experiment is continuously executed until the first successful outcome, the geometric distribution provides the probability spread of the number of unsuccessful attempts preceding this success.

Continuous Distributions:

These pertain to situations where possible results can span a range of continuous outcomes, as opposed to specific, discrete ones. For example, measuring the height of people in a given sample or the time elapsed at a traffic light.

Normal (Gaussian) Distribution: A universally recognized curve in statistical studies. Outcomes nearest to the average are the most probable and dwindle in likelihood as they deviate further. Parameters include its average or mean, μ, and the degree of spread or standard deviation, σ.

Exponential Distribution: Reflecting on the intervals between events distributed according to the Poisson process, they can be depicted using the exponential distribution. This represents the gaps between consecutive occurrences in a Poisson system, where events emerge continuously and without dependency at a fixed rate.

Uniform Distribution: In this model, all possible outcomes within a defined range possess an identical probability.

Picturing the random selection of a number from 1 to 10 is a fitting example, where each number holds the same selection probability.

Beta Distribution: This distribution is adaptable and confined between 0 and 1. Especially valuable when representing fractions or ratios, its form can vary based on its specific parameters.

Gamma Distribution: Commonly associated with wait times between events in the Poisson model, but considering multiple such events. It's flexible and can portray a range of asymmetric distributions.

Practical Implications:

Probability distributions find use in numerous real-world scenarios:

Financial modeling helps in forecasting future market behaviors or fluctuating interest rates.

In logistics and planning, they might depict the frequency of customers at a service counter within a specific period.

For quality assurance, they facilitate predictions about probable defects in a product batch.

In ecological research, they can denote daily precipitation amounts or contaminant levels.

In medical research, distributions could represent a population's vital statistics or the impact of novel treatments.

Unraveling probability distributions is vital for professionals dealing with data and inherent uncertainties. They offer a logical blueprint to portray intrinsic randomness in diverse contexts, empowering experts to make evidence-based determinations. Mastery over these distributions and their attributes enables the analysis of intricate systems, the development of refined predictive tools, and the extraction of insights from ostensibly disorderly data.

Hypothesis testing

Central to the sphere of statistics, hypothesis testing offers a systematic method to make informed decisions based on empirical evidence. Through the juxtaposition of two competing assertions regarding a population metric, researchers can analyze sample data and determine which assertion aligns more closely with their findings, granting the capacity to project these conclusions to a wider population.

Diving into its essence, hypothesis testing centers on assessing two primary statements:

Null Hypothesis (Ho): An initial claim suggesting no noticeable effect or disparity, often seen as a default stance. The objective is often to challenge or refute this claim.

Alternative Hypothesis (H1 or Ha): This denotes the researcher's main contention, positing that a significant effect or discrepancy exists.

Procedure:

The methodology for hypothesis testing unfolds through several organized steps:

Draft the Hypotheses: Begin by defining the null and alternative hypotheses. For example, arguing that a novel medication lacks efficacy versus asserting its significant impact.

Determine the Significance Level (α): Typically set at 0.05, this metric delineates the odds of dismissing the null hypothesis when it's accurate. It represents the investigator's accepted risk.

Identify the Relevant Test: Depending on the data type and the inquiry, opt for an apt statistical test, such as t-tests, chi-squared tests, or ANOVA.

Calculate the Test Statistic: By comparing sample findings with what the null hypothesis predicts, derive the test statistic.

Ascertain the p-value: This metric sheds light on the extremity of the test statistic in relation to the null hypothesis. A diminished p-value suggests that such data would be atypical under the null hypothesis.

Reach a Verdict: If the p-value is beneath the chosen α, the null hypothesis is dismissed, favoring the alternative. If it's greater, there's not enough compelling evidence to discard the null hypothesis.

Potential Misjudgments:

Mistakes are inherent in hypothesis testing:

Type I Error (False Positive): This emerges when the null hypothesis is inaccurately rejected, even though it holds true. The likelihood of this error is represented by α.

Type II Error (False Negative): This happens when the null hypothesis is mistakenly upheld when, in reality, the alternative is accurate. Denoted by β, a test's power $(1 - \beta)$ represents the likelihood of correctly discarding the null hypothesis when the alternative is accurate.

Applications in the Field:

Hypothesis testing finds relevance in various domains:

Medical Investigations: Prior to endorsing novel therapeutic approaches, hypothesis testing is pivotal in determining their superiority over existing treatments or inert substitutes.

Corporate Choices: Firms utilize hypothesis testing to gauge the impact of marketing initiatives, evaluate procedural alterations, or assess new product prospects.

Economic Studies: Economists leverage these tests to identify correlations between variables or corroborate theoretical assertions.

Assurance of Quality: In the realm of manufacturing, hypothesis testing ascertains if product batches fulfill designated quality benchmarks.

Points of Caution:

Although a formidable tool, hypothesis testing demands discerning usage:

Magnitude of Effect: A notable p-value doesn't necessarily signify practical relevance. Gauging the magnitude of the effect is crucial for assessing the real-world consequences.

Concurrent Testing: Undertaking multiple hypothesis tests augments the probability of detecting a significant result by mere happenstance. Techniques like the Bonferroni correction can temper this risk.

Underlying Presumptions: Each test bears inherent assumptions, such as data distribution characteristics. Disregarding these can undermine the test's integrity.

To encapsulate, hypothesis testing serves as a stalwart instrument enabling decisions anchored in data. By offering a refined protocol to assess evidence and derive population-based conclusions from sample data, it furnishes professionals from various sectors with the apparatus to render insightful, fact-based determinations. However, its efficacy is contingent upon its judicious application and cognizance of its boundaries.

Chapter Five

Data Pre-processing and Transformation

Data normalization and standardization

Navigating the multifaceted domain of data science, it becomes evident that the treatment of data before any analysis holds tremendous significance. At the heart of this preparation lie two essential techniques: data normalization and standardization. Though they share the goal of refining the scale of numerical variables, they follow distinct methods and have varied implications.

On Data Normalization:

Normalization is the technique that adjusts numeric data points to fit within a common range, frequently between 0 and 1. This method is pivotal in aligning the scales of different attributes, ensuring that no singular feature unduly sways the outcome of an algorithm due to its larger scale.

The prevalent formula for normalization is:

$$\text{Normalized Value} = \frac{\text{Value} - \text{Lowest Value}}{\text{Highest Value} - \text{Lowest Value}}$$

For illustration, let's take a dataset with house prices and the number of bedrooms. Prices might span hundreds of thousands, whereas bedroom numbers would likely be between 1 and 10. By normalizing these features, you ensure each attribute has an equitable impact, especially vital for algorithms like K-means clustering where distance computations matter.

Regarding Data Standardization:

Standardization, also known as z-score normalization, reshapes data such that it has a mean (μ) of 0 and a standard deviation (σ) of 1. While the distribution's overall form remains unchanged, the resulting mean and spread conform to a standard normal distribution.

The formula used is:

$$\text{Standardized Value} = \frac{\text{Value} - \text{Average}}{\text{Standard Deviation}}$$

Such a procedure is pivotal when data exhibits a Gaussian distribution. Models such as Support Vector Machines (SVM) or Linear Regression, which rely on weight coefficients, especially benefit from standardization to avoid scale-induced distortions.

Choosing Between the Two:

Deciding between normalization and standardization hinges on the data's nature and the specific algorithm in use.

Nature of Distribution: Gaussian or near-Gaussian distributed features or algorithms that assume Gaussian characteristics (like linear regression) often benefit more from standardization. Otherwise, normalization might be better suited.

Algorithm Characteristics: For models like K-NN, SVM, or neural networks where scale matters, normalization or standardization is indispensable. Yet, for algorithms like decision trees, this isn't always the case.

Expert Insight: In some situations, industry knowledge guides the choice. For instance, in image analysis, pixel values are typically normalized between 0 and 1 for certain deep learning algorithms.

Ease of Interpretation: While standardization maintains the original distribution, aiding in understanding, normalization, with its confined range, can be more intuitive for visualization purposes.

Challenges to Consider:

Outliers: Both methods can be swayed by extreme values. A significant outlier can lead to compressed scaled values. Utilizing robust scalers that pivot around medians can be a remedy.

Data Evolution: As datasets grow or change, previously applied scales may become obsolete. It emphasizes the need for periodic reassessment and potential adjustments.

Loss of Authentic Scale: Post-transformation, data deviates from its inherent scale. This can be a hurdle, especially when explaining outcomes to those less acquainted with technical intricacies.

In essence, both normalization and standardization are invaluable tools in the data scientist's toolkit. Their careful application can profoundly enhance the efficacy and precision of analytical endeavors. However, their effectiveness lies in their informed use, underscoring the significance of comprehending the data's nature, the model's requirements, and the broader analytical goals.

Handling missing data

In the intricate landscape of data analysis and predictive modeling, one often confronts datasets riddled with absent or incomplete entries. Such voids, if inadequately addressed, can undermine analytical quality, skewing outcomes or rendering them non-representative. The reasons for data omissions are diverse—be it inadvertent data entry lapses or intentional survey non-responses. The central challenge revolves not merely around patching these gaps, but discerning their root cause and adopting the appropriate remedy.

Triggers for Data Absence:

Data omissions typically fall into one of three classifications:

Completely Random Missing Data (MCAR): Here, a variable's missing nature is unrelated to both observed and hidden data. An illustrative case might be intermittent data loss from sporadic sensor malfunctions.

Randomly Missing Data (MAR): Missingness hinges on other observable data but isn't directly connected to the absent data's intrinsic values. A fitting scenario might be a survey where younger individuals more frequently withhold their earnings, yet the absent earnings data isn't linked to the actual earnings.

Non-random Missing Data (MNAR): The likelihood of an omission correlates with the missing value itself. For instance, in health surveys, patients with more severe symptoms might be less forthcoming.

Recognizing the underlying cause of data absence is pivotal. It determines the aptness of imputation techniques and shapes the credibility of ensuing interpretations.

Tactics to Counter Data Omissions:

Exclusion Approaches:

Full Entry Exclusion: This tactic discards any record with even a single data omission. While it ensures the authenticity of the remaining data, it risks squandering valuable data, particularly if missing entries are pervasive.

Variable Pair Exclusion: Predominantly employed in correlation analyses, this method harnesses as many entries as feasible. When two variables are assessed for correlation, only paired entries with complete data for both are considered.

Substitution Approaches:

Average/Subgroup/Subtype Replacement: Here, the vacant spot is replaced with either the average (for continuous datasets) or the most frequent value (for categorical datasets). However, this can inadvertently diminish data variability.

Predictive Regression Replacement: This exploits other attributes to estimate and substitute missing entries, presupposing a linear interrelation between variables.

Neighbor-based Estimation (KNN): This locates 'k' close matches within the dataset to the incomplete record and computes either an average or a central tendency from these neighbors for replacement.

Sophisticated Substitution Techniques:

Iterative Estimation: Rather than a single value substitution, this method predicts several potential values, generating multiple filled datasets. Analysis across these offers a more balanced conclusion.

Time-bound Estimations: Pertinent for datasets across time, this technique relies on known entries to deduce a missing value within (interpolation) or beyond (extrapolation) the known range.

Pattern-driven Methods: Advanced algorithms, including the Expectation-Maximization approach or Bayesian inferences, can be harnessed for replacement, anchored in the identified data patterns.

Particular Measures for Discrete Data: For non-continuous variables, an alternative category representing "absent" can be constituted, allowing the dataset to recognize and work with these voids as distinctive information.

Potential Pitfalls and Deliberations:

Inclinations: All approaches carry a potential bias risk. While direct exclusion can curtail dataset breadth, jeopardizing statistical vigor, substitutions can alter inherent data patterns.

Operational Demands: Techniques like the KNN or iterative estimations can be demanding on computational resources, a significant consideration for voluminous datasets.

Inherent Assumptions: Each technique rests on foundational suppositions about the dataset. Overlooking these can result in skewed interpretations.

In Summation:

Addressing data omissions is a nuanced endeavor that blends methodological rigor with domain discernment. The most effective strategy typically unfolds in stages—initial exploratory examinations to gauge the nature of absences, the application of befitting replacement methods, and subsequent validations via domain expertise and ancillary data repositories, ensuring analyses are both rigorous and dependable.

Categorical data encoding

The world of data analytics and modeling often requires translating human-understandable data into a format machines can easily digest. Among the most prominent types of data requiring such transformation is categorical data, which is inherently non-numerical. Encoding these types of data into machine-readable formats is a pivotal step in data preprocessing. The choice of encoding method often depends on the specific characteristics of the data and the intended application.

Distinguishing Types of Categorical Data:

Broadly, we can identify categorical data as:

Ordinal Data: Such data has a clear sequence or hierarchy. Consider, for example, the gradation of "low", "medium", and "high".

Nominal Data: Without any implicit ranking, this data type includes categories like "red", "blue", or "green", where no value inherently outweighs another.

Common Encoding Mechanisms:

Label Encoding:

By assigning a unique number to each category, this method is simple and efficient. It is particularly effective for ordinal data due to the numerical sequence it creates. However, its application on nominal data can unintentionally imply a sequence, which can mislead some algorithms.

One-Hot Encoding:

Each category spawns a new binary column, indicating its presence or absence. This method avoids implying false hierarchy, making it ideal for nominal data. A downside, however, is the increase in data dimensions, which can pose computational challenges.

Binary Encoding:

This approach first assigns numerical labels to categories, which are then converted to binary code. This hybrid method can still imply a degree of hierarchy but is more space-efficient than one-hot encoding.

Frequency or Count Encoding:

Categories are replaced with their occurrence count or their proportional frequency. This is a space-conservative method but can lead to potential issues if two categories share similar counts.

Target (Mean) Encoding:

For supervised learning tasks, categories can be encoded based on the target variable's mean. While powerful, it can overfit smaller datasets. It's essential to employ regularization techniques to mitigate this.

Embedding Layers:

Within deep learning paradigms, embeddings can represent categorical variables. These dense vectors, learned during training, can encapsulate intricate category relationships, especially when dealing with large category sets.

Key Considerations:

Dimensionality: Encoding, especially one-hot, can expand the feature set, leading to computational demands and potential overfitting.

Collinearity: Certain encoding methods can result in multicollinear features, problematic for some models. Techniques like dimensionality reduction can be beneficial in these scenarios.

Risk of Data Leakage: Techniques, notably target encoding, can leak data if the entire dataset is utilized for encoding. Proper partitioning of data and cross-validation is crucial.

Algorithmic Differences: Algorithms like decision trees may handle label encoding of nominal data adequately, while models like linear regression or neural networks may struggle with the implied hierarchy.

Consistency Post-Deployment: Once a model is in production, the encoding scheme must remain consistent for any incoming new data. Maintaining an encoding blueprint or automated pipeline is essential.

Closing Remarks:

Encoding categorical data is an indispensable facet of data preprocessing. Given the multitude of available techniques, comprehending the data's nature, the specific problem, and the selected algorithm's nuances is crucial. Properly chosen and applied encoding not only elevates model performance but also facilitates smoother analytics, yielding dependable and insightful results.

Chapter Six

Machine Learning Basics

Overview of machine learning

Machine learning, an essential pillar of artificial intelligence, represents a revolutionary approach to computational problem-solving and decision-making across diverse sectors. By empowering systems to enhance their capabilities through data without explicit instructions, machine learning signifies a transformative phase in computational methodologies.

Fundamentals and Tenets:

Machine learning fundamentally aims to identify and exploit patterns embedded within data. The overarching ambition is to base predictions or conclusions on these inferred patterns. This approach stands in contrast to classical computational techniques that rely on meticulously designed logic. In machine learning, the patterns are learned from the data itself.

Categories of Learning:

Machine learning can be broadly dissected based on the nature of the learning mechanism, primarily:

Supervised Learning: Predominantly used, in this approach, algorithms are fed labeled data, encompassing both the input and the expected outcome. The algorithm then aspires to discern a relationship between the input and the output. Regression and classification are illustrative examples.

Unsupervised Learning: Here, in the absence of predefined labels, the algorithm strives to unveil underlying structures or relationships within the dataset. Techniques like clustering and dimensionality reduction are emblematic of this approach.

Reinforcement Learning: In this dynamic setup, an entity or 'agent' interacts with its surroundings, performing actions and receiving subsequent feedback, either as rewards or penalties. The agent's objective is to optimize these rewards over prolonged interactions, learning optimal actions through experiences.

Central Elements:

A typical machine learning project traverses through stages that include data acquisition, preprocessing, model choice, training, validation, evaluation, and deployment. In this context, 'model' denotes the specific algorithmic structure or architecture selected, while 'training' signifies the phase where this model absorbs patterns from data.

Balancing Complexity:

In the machine learning landscape, the balance between bias and variance is critical. Models that are excessively intricate might demonstrate stellar performance on known data but falter with unfamiliar data due to a phenomenon called overfitting. Techniques such as L1 and L2 regularization, dropout strategies, and early termination are implemented to curtail this over-elaboration and ensure models remain versatile.

Performance Indicators:

Measuring a machine learning model's proficiency is of paramount importance. Depending on the task's nature, metrics like accuracy, precision, recall, F1 score, and mean squared error, among others, become pivotal in assessing a model's potency.

Collective Approaches:

Acknowledging that a singular model might not be optimal for every scenario, collective or ensemble techniques merge outputs from multiple models to render a consolidated outcome. Strategies like bagging and boosting are renowned ensemble methodologies that have proven instrumental in numerous machine-learning challenges.

Neural Architectures and Deep Learning:

Drawing inspiration from biological neural structures, artificial neural networks form a subset of machine learning models. When these networks possess multiple intertwined layers, facilitating the hierarchical learning of features, they transition into what's known as deep learning. While they have been conceptualized for some time, recent advancements in computational capacities and the influx of massive datasets have elevated deep learning's prominence in tasks like image processing and voice recognition.

Contemporary Scenario and Hurdles:

While machine learning, augmented by deep learning, has achieved commendable breakthroughs, embodying innovations from smart assistants to self-driving cars, hurdles persist. The opacity or the 'black box' characteristic of models, predominantly deep neural networks, is a concern. Challenges surrounding inadvertent biases, fairness, and ethical considerations are gaining traction. Assuring resilience, dependability, and security, especially in hostile conditions, is an ongoing research domain.

Final Remarks:

Undoubtedly, machine learning is a defining technological marvel of our times. Its utility spans sectors, ranging from medical diagnostics to financial forecasting. As we continue to generate and navigate through vast data oceans, machine learning's role in deriving insights and facilitating informed decisions will only magnify. Nevertheless, its ethical and responsible deployment remains a priority to fully harness its extensive advantages.

Supervised vs. unsupervised learning

Machine learning encompasses a broad spectrum of methodologies, but two primary paradigms emerge supervised and unsupervised learning. Each operates with distinct foundational concepts and is tailored for different types of tasks. Recognizing the nuances between these approaches can greatly illuminate the mechanics of algorithmic learning and optimize their application.

Supervised Learning: An Overview

Supervised learning is predicated on the notion of instructive guidance. In this framework, algorithms derive insights from a

In Conclusion

In essence, while supervised and unsupervised learning approaches present unique perspectives and techniques, understanding their individual strengths and distinctions ensures their optimal deployment. As the data landscape continues to evolve, the strategic application of these paradigms will be pivotal in gleaning actionable insights and fostering sectoral advancements.

Model evaluation metrics

Assessing the performance of machine learning models is of paramount importance. A high-quality model isn't just one that operates well on its training set, but one that adapts effectively to unseen data. Therefore, we utilize a range of metrics to gauge the reliability, accuracy, and overall effectiveness of these models. This piece provides insight into these crucial metrics, highlighting their relevance and application in various scenarios.

1. Accuracy

This widely recognized metric calculates the proportion of correct predictions made by the model. The formula is:

$$\text{Accuracy} = \frac{\text{Correct Predictions}}{\text{Total Predictions Made}}$$

Nevertheless, accuracy can sometimes provide a skewed perspective, especially in datasets where one class is significantly overrepresented.

2. Precision and Recall

For binary classifiers, these two are fundamental:

Precision: It's the fraction of relevant instances among the retrieved instances. In other words:

$$\text{Precision} = \frac{\text{Correctly Predicted Positives}}{\text{Total Predicted Positives}}$$

Recall (or Sensitivity): This metric tells us what proportion of actual positives was identified correctly.

$$\text{Recall} = \frac{\text{Correctly Predicted Positives}}{\text{Correctly Predicted Positives} + \text{Missed Positives}}$$

3. F1-Score

The F1-Score amalgamates precision and recall into one metric. It's particularly beneficial in cases of uneven class distribution.

$$\text{F1 Score} = 2 \times \frac{\text{Precision x Recall}}{\text{Precision} + \text{Recall}}$$

4. ROC-AUC

The Receiver Operating Characteristic (ROC) curve and the Area Under the Curve (AUC) together offer insights into a model's discriminative power. An ideal model has an AUC of 1, while a model relying on pure chance would score 0.5.

5. Mean Absolute Error (MAE)

Predominantly for regression models, MAE is the average of the absolute differences between predictions and actual values.

$$\text{MAE} = \frac{1}{n} \sum |actual - predicted|$$

6. Mean Squared Error (MSE)

Another key metric for regression, MSE emphasizes larger errors by squaring them prior to averaging.

$$\text{MSE} = \frac{1}{n} \sum (actual - predicted)^2$$

7. Root Mean Squared Error (RMSE)

RMSE, the square root of MSE, conveys the standard deviation of the discrepancies between what's observed and what's predicted.

$$\text{RMSE} = \sqrt{\frac{1}{n} \sum (actual - predicted)^2}$$

8. Confusion Matrix

This tabulated representation breaks down the entirety of potential outcomes in classification. It's not only useful for gauging model success but also helps identify the nature of errors.

9. Log Loss

Log Loss measures classifier performance while penalizing wrong classifications. The closer the log loss is to 0, the better the model.

10. Cohen's Kappa

This metric indicates how much better the predictions are than a classification done by random chance, especially when there's a class imbalance.

11. R-squared (Coefficient of Determination)

In regression scenarios, R-squared reveals the percentage of the variance in the outcome variable that the independent variables explain collectively.

To wrap up, while we have a plethora of metrics at our disposal, model assessment is about judiciously choosing the right ones, keeping in line with the dataset, business context, and the problem's nature. These tools equip data professionals to differentiate between models, iterating upon them for better real-world efficacy. Yet, it's essential to interpret these metrics within the broader context of the given task.

Chapter Seven

Deep Learning and Neural Networks

Introduction to neural networks

Within the broad domain of artificial intelligence (AI), neural networks have emerged as a significant component. These are computational frameworks, inspired by the intricate workings of the human brain's biological neural networks. Their primary objective is to discern patterns. This is achieved by processing sensory data and facilitating machine interpretation, categorization, or raw input clustering. The patterns they identify are fundamentally numeric and require all real-world inputs, such as images, sounds, text, or time series, to be converted into vectors.

Inspired by Biology

The term "neural network" clearly hints at its biological roots. In the human brain, neurons serve as interconnected nerve cells, playing a vital role in computation, cognition, and memory storage. Activated by various stimuli, they transmit data to neighboring neurons via synapses. Similarly, an artificial neural network comprises connected nodes or "neurons" categorized into different layers: the input layer, several hidden layers, and the output layer.

The Inner Workings

Each inter-node connection possesses a specific weight, which is fine-tuned during the learning process. Along with a bias, these weights are instrumental in the network's decision-making and data-processing capabilities. Each node processes the input using a combination of weighted sums and a subsequent transformation through an activation function to generate an output.

These activation functions bring non-linearity to the network. This non-linearity is crucial, enabling the network to learn from its mistakes and adjust accordingly – a fundamental aspect of tasks such as classification and regression. Some common activation functions include the sigmoid, ReLU (rectified linear unit), and hyperbolic tangent (tanh).

Educating the Neural Network

The essence of training a neural network lies in identifying optimal weight sets to make precise predictions. Initially, weights are typically assigned randomly. This is followed by forward propagation, wherein the network formulates its prediction. The accuracy of this prediction is assessed using a loss function, which measures the difference between the predicted and actual values.

The critical step of backpropagation then updates the network's weights to minimize this loss. It calculates the loss function's gradient with respect to each weight using the chain rule, a fundamental component of optimization strategies like gradient descent.

Diverse Neural Networks and Their Applications

Neural networks can vary in depth, referring to the number of layers they possess. Those with numerous layers are termed "deep neural networks." This depth is foundational to Deep

Learning, a machine learning subset where such networks have transformed fields like speech and image recognition.

Several neural network variants cater to specific applications. For instance, Convolutional Neural Networks (CNNs) are exceptional for image processing due to their grid-oriented data processing capability. In contrast, Recurrent Neural Networks (RNNs) are better suited for sequential data such as natural language or time series, as they incorporate loops to maintain information.

Overcoming Challenges

Despite their remarkable capabilities, neural networks present certain challenges. They demand substantial data and computing resources. Overfitting is a common concern, where the model's performance on training data is stellar but falters on new data. Strategies such as dropout or regularization can help counter this.

Furthermore, their decision-making processes, while sophisticated, lack transparency, leading them to be termed "black boxes." Current research, involving methods like SHAP (SHapley Additive exPlanations) and LIME (Local Interpretable Model-agnostic Explanations), aims to enhance their interpretability.

In Summary

Neural networks epitomize the union of biology and computational science, capturing the attention of both academic researchers and industry experts. As we navigate the AI-driven landscape, mastering these intricate tools is paramount. However, their utility hinges not only on technological advancements but also on a comprehensive understanding of their potential, constraints, and the discernment to utilize them aptly.

Basics of deep learning architectures

The realm of artificial intelligence (AI) has been dramatically reshaped by deep learning, a specialized branch of machine learning. This transformation is largely attributed to complex architectures that aspire to mimic human cognitive and decision-making processes in a myriad of applications. Whether it's discerning human speech or detecting objects in images, these architectures utilize vast data volumes, navigating through layers of interlinked nodes, to discern patterns that often elude conventional algorithms.

The Building Block: The Neuron

To truly grasp the nuances of deep architectures, one must start with the fundamental computational component: the neuron. Drawing parallels to the biological neurons in our brains, artificial neurons accept multiple inputs, process them via weights, biases, and an activation function, and then generate an output. These weights and biases, which start as random values, undergo iterative adjustments, enhancing the network's efficiency in tasks like categorizing data or forecasting trends.

The Stratified Structure

The term "deep" in deep learning is a nod to the "depth" or the multiple layers it encompasses. Broadly, these layers are:

Input Layer: The primary layer that introduces raw data. Each node here generally corresponds to a single feature or variable in the data.

Hidden Layers: Positioned between the input and output layers, these layers—often numerous in number—process the data, refining it step-by-step. Each subsequent layer is tasked with identifying particular features, with the deeper layers recognizing more intricate attributes.

Output Layer: This concluding layer presents the final outcome, be it a category, a projection, or any other intended result.

Renowned Deep Learning Structures

Feedforward Neural Networks (FNN): This straightforward structure ensures unidirectional data flow—from its entry point (the input layer), via hidden layers, to its exit (the output layer), without any loops or recurrent paths.

Convolutional Neural Networks (CNNs): Tailored for structured data like images, CNNs incorporate convolutional layers to sieve data, pooling layers to diminish dimensionality, and densely connected layers for making determinations. By inherently learning spatial feature hierarchies, they excel in tasks like image categorization.

Recurrent Neural Networks (RNNs): Distinct from FNNs, RNNs have inherent loops, ensuring data retention. This quality suits them for sequential datasets like stock market trends or texts. Yet, standard RNNs grapple with sustaining long-term dependencies, facing hurdles like gradients that vanish or explode. Variations such as Long Short-Term Memory (LSTM) and Gated Recurrent Units (GRU) have been formulated to surmount these impediments.

Generative Adversarial Networks (GANs): Consisting of dual neural networks—the generator and the discriminator—GANs operate in concert. While the generator crafts data, the discriminator critiques its genuineness. This competitive interaction facilitates the generator in fabricating data nearly indistinguishable from genuine samples, making it suitable for creative tasks.

Autoencoders: Primarily applied for data condensation and eliminating noise. An autoencoder comprises two segments: an encoder, responsible for data compression, and a decoder, tasked with data reconstruction. The goal is to have minimal variance between original and restored data.

Transformer Models: Predominantly employed in linguistic tasks, transformers eschew loops, focusing instead on attention mechanisms. This modus operandi enables them to ascertain the relevance of distinct data portions. For instance, the BERT model has set benchmarks in numerous language-related challenges.

Training and Predicaments

To train deep learning models, a process is adopted: forward propagation (letting data traverse the network), determining a loss function (measuring deviation between expected and actual results), and backpropagation (tweaking weights and biases through optimization strategies).

However, challenges persist. Requisites like voluminous datasets, significant computational resources, potential model overfitting, and the opaque nature of decision-making processes remain areas for contemplation and ongoing study.

Looking Forward

The trajectory of deep learning is marked by continual advancement. While the structures discussed above have elevated AI's capabilities, they merely scratch the surface. Ongoing investigations, breakthroughs, and a richer comprehension of these models' intricacies promise to set new benchmarks in AI, widening its scope and potential.

Applications in data science

The expansive realm of data science has ushered in a new era, acting as the nexus between raw information and actionable decisions. As the volume of data we produce surges, data science's influence broadens, leading to a multitude of applications that touch various facets of our lives and reshape traditional business operations. Here's a deep dive into several critical applications of data science across diverse domains.

1. Healthcare and Life Sciences

Data-driven innovations have significantly enriched healthcare. By using predictive analytics, healthcare professionals can foresee disease outbreaks, advance the quality of patient care, and anticipate hospital admission rates, ensuring judicious use of resources. Moreover, the confluence of genomics and data analytics facilitates treatments tailored to individual genetic structures.

2. Retail and E-commerce

For the retail industry, data science is a beacon guiding their strategies. By scrutinizing customer buying behaviours and historical purchases, retailers can make informed decisions on inventory management. Online retail platforms harness algorithms to offer product suggestions, elevating the user's shopping experience and propelling sales.

3. Finance and Banking

The financial realm leans heavily on data science for risk management and identifying fraudulent activities. By studying transactional behaviours, potential anomalies that hint at fraud can be detected. Additionally, the algorithms that evaluate an individual's fiscal behaviour to determine credit scores are deeply rooted in data analytics.

4. Transportation and Logistics

The logistics sector is fine-tuned with the insights derived from data science. Factors like real-time traffic data, impending weather conditions, and vehicle health are analyzed to streamline operations. Platforms offering shared rides use this data to pair drivers with passengers, decide dynamic pricing, and recommend the best routes.

5. Energy Sector

Forecasting energy consumption is pivotal to ensuring uninterrupted power supply. By juxtaposing historical usage, meteorological forecasts, and significant events, algorithms can deduce power consumption trends. In the renewable energy sphere, data insights assist in pinpointing the ideal spots for setting up solar panels or wind turbines.

6. Entertainment and Media

Streaming platforms such as Netflix or Spotify exploit data science to decode user inclinations. This decoding, derived from users' viewing or listening history, aids in creating personalized content recommendations. Film studios also leverage analytics to gauge the potential popularity of their releases based on factors like actor fanbase, past viewing trends, and script content.

7. Manufacturing and Production

In the manufacturing landscape, quality control and maintenance predictions owe their precision to data science. Real-time production metrics allow for immediate identification of potential issues, ensuring product consistency. Meanwhile, sensor data and historical maintenance records forecast when equipment might need attention, reducing operational halts.

8. Agriculture and Farming

Modern agriculture is steeped in data insights. Using sensors and satellite imagery, it's possible to monitor myriad factors like soil vitality, crop progression, and potential pest threats. Such granular data enables timely interventions, such as adjusting irrigation or deploying protective measures against pests.

9. Public Policy and Governance

Data science plays a pivotal role in public governance and policy formation. By dissecting socio-economic datasets, areas that need immediate attention, whether it's health, infrastructure, or education, can be identified. Additionally, during electoral cycles, analyzing sentiments on social platforms can offer a glimpse into public sentiment, aiding in campaign strategies.

10. Research and Academia

In the academic sphere, data science tools offer a fresh lens to view intricate datasets, revealing patterns that might escape conventional research methods. Be it deducing climatic shifts from historical weather data or interpreting societal trends from extensive demographic datasets, data science accelerates the pace of breakthroughs.

Conclusion

The multifaceted applications of data science span sectors and continue to evolve. As our prowess in data collection and interpretation amplifies, so will our ability to harness its potential for diverse applications. Evidently, data science is more than a trending term; it's a transformative force pushing industries and society into an era steered by data.

Chapter Eight

Natural Language Processing (NLP)

Basics of NLP

Natural Language Processing, often abbreviated as NLP, serves as a critical juncture between computer science, artificial intelligence (AI), and the intricate subtleties of human communication. It endeavors to teach machines the ability to understand, decode, and produce human language, enhancing the fluidity of human-machine communication. This piece delves into the essential principles of NLP, its aspirations, and the array of methods utilized to meet these aims.

Primary Goals of NLP:

At its core, NLP is about empowering machines to grasp, decode, and emit human language in ways that resonate with human understanding and context. The pivotal goals encompass:

Text Interpretation: NLP's foundational task is to sift through copious text amounts, unraveling its construct and significance. This might span from grasping the emotion behind a statement to sifting out critical details.

Linguistic Translation: Shifting text or spoken words from one dialect to another while retaining its context and nuances remains a central NLP function. Prime examples can be seen in tools like Google Translate.

Voice Recognition: Transcribing spoken words into text and deducing the underlying purpose is another area NLP seeks to master.

Linguistic Creation: NLP isn't just about comprehension and translation; it also aims to let machines craft human-like textual content, from forming emails to devising chatbots or generating narratives.

Foundational NLP Methods:

Achieving the vast scope of NLP mandates an amalgamation of nuanced techniques, blending linguistic insights with the prowess of machine learning and deep learning frameworks. Noteworthy methods include:

Tokenization: This process divides text into smaller fragments, typically words or syllables, termed tokens. Such tokens act as foundational units for textual scrutiny.

Part-of-Speech Labeling: Within this method, words are categorized based on their linguistic role, such as pronouns, verbs, descriptors, and so on. This aids in understanding the textual framework and word interrelationships.

Named Entity Categorization (NEC): NEC's goal is to pinpoint and classify entities in text, allocating them to set groups like individual names, corporate identities, geographical locations, time markers, quantities, or financial metrics.

Relational Parsing: This reveals the interconnectedness between words, assisting in demystifying sentence structure and the functions of various words.

Semantic Exploration: Beyond mere word arrangement (syntax), semantics dive into word meanings. Through semantic exploration, the intent behind words and phrases across diverse scenarios is unraveled.

Word Vectorization: This translates words into vector formats, encapsulating their semantic essence. Semantically similar words tend to be proximal in this vector space, letting machines assess word likeness and application.

Thematic Extraction: Predominantly used in text mining, this technique discerns themes within a body of text. Systems like Latent Dirichlet Allocation (LDA) are commonly used for such extraction.

Emotive Analysis: This technique determines the emotion or mood contained in a text segment, segregating it as positive, negative, or indifferent. It's particularly useful in realms like brand analysis and social media trend tracking.

NLP's Roadblocks:

While NLP has achieved remarkable progress, it's not devoid of challenges. Human language, with its inherent ambiguities, local nuances, and cultural disparities, presents a daunting task for machines. Words with varied interpretations (homonyms) or phrases that rely heavily on context often puzzle NLP systems. For instance, the term "bank" could signify a monetary entity or a river's edge.

Moreover, the fluid nature of languages, which continuously birth new terms, colloquial expressions, and evolving usages, means NLP tools must be ever-evolving.

Wrapping Up:

NLP stands as a beacon, narrowing the communication divide between humans and our digital counterparts. As advancements surge and techniques mature, we're steadily progressing toward an era where machines do not just decode human language but engage in it, elevating our digital interactions to new heights.

Text processing techniques

In today's data-centric era, proficiency in managing and interpreting massive text volumes stands as a cornerstone skill within data science. Given that text often comes as unstructured data, it demands a unique set of strategies to distill valuable insights. Text processing, in essence, is about transforming raw textual content into a format primed for analytical endeavors. This discussion navigates through the key approaches utilized in text processing to set the stage for insightful data analysis.

Tokenization:

At its core, tokenization dissects a text flow into constituent words, phrases, or other salient elements termed as tokens. These tokens act as foundational pillars for grasping context or implied meanings. For instance, dividing "Data science is evolving" results in: ["Data", "science", "is", "evolving"].

Excluding Stop Words:

Certain words like "and", "of", or "with" often don't amplify the core message in text analytics and are thus commonly omitted.

By doing so, the data footprint is minimized, paving the way for streamlined processes like thematic modeling.

Stemming:

This technique trims words to their rudimentary form. Words like "running", "runs", and "runner" could all boil down to "run". Stemming's objective is to collate related words under a singular banner.

Lemmatization:

In contrast to stemming, lemmatization leverages a vocabulary and morphological analysis to reduce words to their genuine or canonical form. "better" might be traced back to "good". While more resource-intensive, its precision is often superior, especially for context-sensitive scenarios.

Tagging Words by Role:

This involves tagging tokens with their grammatical role, such as "noun", "verb", or "adjective". Recognizing a word's role can be instrumental in deciphering its intended implication.

Identifying Named Entities (NER):

This method is about pinpointing and categorizing named entities in text into predefined buckets like "individuals", "groups", "places", and so forth. It's invaluable for extracting systematic data from chaotic textual masses.

TF-IDF Calculation:

A metric extensively used in text mining, TF-IDF gauges the relevance of a word to a document within a collection. Words appearing frequently in a single document but rarely across multiple documents are given higher prominence.

Bag of Words (BoW) Model:

A rudimentary text representation, where a textual snippet is viewed as an unordered word collection, disregarding syntactic rules. It finds frequent application in document categorization, utilizing word occurrence rates as indicators.

Word Embeddings:

Dense vector representations encapsulating word meanings based on the surrounding context. Renowned models include Word2Vec and GloVe. Such embeddings can discern semantic word relationships, optimizing performance across various linguistic tasks.

Uniform Text Representation:

It's about homogenizing all text elements within a document, for instance, transitioning all characters to lowercase, or omitting punctuations. This process enforces consistency and simplifies the data structure.

n-grams:

An n-gram is a consecutive word sequence from a given text sample. Single words are unigrams, pairs are bigrams, and so on. Implementing n-grams can assist in capturing phrase context, proving invaluable in sentiment deduction tasks.

Pattern Matching via Regular Expressions:

Regular expressions are potent tools for identifying and extracting textual patterns. They're fundamental for tasks like data retrieval or transformation, such as pinpointing email IDs or web addresses.

Text Grouping and Classification:

After refining and formatting text data (using methods like TF-IDF or word embeddings), various algorithmic solutions can be employed for categorizing (spam vs. genuine) or for clustering similar content.

To sum it up, text processing lays the groundwork for myriad applications in linguistic processing and machine learning. Whether the goal is sentiment deduction, topic identification, or document categorization, these strategies guarantee that the raw textual content is remodeled for deeper analytics. As the influx of unstructured textual data escalates in our digital epoch, these techniques become ever more paramount for data aficionados.

Applications of NLP in data science

The exponential surge in unstructured text data in today's digital environment highlights the indispensable role of Natural Language Processing (NLP) in the sphere of data science. Acting as the interface between human linguistics and computer algorithms, NLP paves the way for machines to comprehend, evaluate, and engage with human language. As we progress further into this digital epoch, it's crucial for entities ranging from businesses to governments to recognize and harness the multifaceted capabilities of NLP. This exposition sheds light on the diverse ways NLP is employed within the data science domain.

Sentiment Analysis:

A flagship application of NLP, sentiment analysis provides invaluable insights into public perception regarding products, services, or brand-related discussions in the digital sphere. This instant feedback system empowers businesses to fine-tune strategies based on prevailing audience sentiments.

Chatbots and Virtual Assistants:

Embedded with advanced NLP modules, these digital mechanisms are reshaping online user interactions and customer service paradigms. From Cortana to Google Assistant, these tools mimic human interaction, offering timely replies, and amplifying user engagement.

Machine Translation:

In our globally connected world, linguistic gaps can impede seamless interaction. NLP-empowered solutions, such as DeepL, help overcome these barriers, facilitating instant translation and promoting uninterrupted cross-linguistic exchanges.

Information Retrieval:

At their core, search engines are masterpieces of information extraction. Advanced NLP techniques refine search outcomes, ensuring users find precisely what they seek with minimal effort.

Document Summarization:

With an avalanche of information available, the ability to condense extended content into succinct summaries is invaluable. NLP-driven algorithms can fashion both pinpointed and generalized summaries, catering to rapid information assimilation.

Topic Modeling:

For expansive text repositories, pinpointing dominant themes is essential. NLP tools, such as Non-Negative Matrix Factorization (NMF), assist in unveiling core topics, and facilitating content sorting and suggestions.

Named Entity Recognition (NER):

NER tools discern and categorize specific entities (like locations, dates, or companies) in text. Its utility spans various sectors, from enhancing data management to aiding in swiftly identifying key data points.

Speech Recognition:

Voice-responsive systems, spanning voice searches to smart home controls, utilize NLP to transcribe voice to text, interpret it, and act accordingly.

Text Classification and Categorization:

Ranging from designating emails to appropriate folders to organizing news articles by themes, NLP-driven algorithms enable methodical segmentation of textual assets based on set parameters.

Optical Character Recognition (OCR):

Enhanced by NLP, OCR tools can transcribe images containing text (typed or handwritten) into digital text. This finds use in digitizing age-old manuscripts, facilitating data entry tasks, or even identifying automobile registration details.

Autocomplete and Predictive Typing:

Modern text interfaces leverage NLP to anticipate subsequent words in a user's typing sequence, making typing swifter and more intuitive.

Ad Targeting:

Organizations can customize ad campaigns based on content produced by users and their sentiments. NLP helps decode user inclinations, refining ad accuracy and bolstering user interaction.

Content Recommendation:

Platforms such as Amazon Prime or Apple Music tap into NLP to assess user patterns and feedback. This facilitates the suggestion of movies, tracks, or reads that resonate with user tastes.

Medical Applications:

In the medical realm, NLP solutions process clinical records, academic publications, or patient notes to assist in diagnostics, treatment enhancement, and administrative fluidity.

Legal and Compliance Monitoring:

For legal purposes, NLP assists in navigating vast document repositories, flagging potential compliance deviations, or extracting critical legal terms, making legal scrutiny more efficient.

In summary, NLP is the compass guiding us through the labyrinth of textual data, unveiling insights and streamlining operations. Its utility in data science is bound only by our creative boundaries. As our computational prowess escalates and NLP methodologies become more intricate, the future beckons with even more transformative applications in data science.

Chapter Nine

Time Series Analysis

What is a time series?

Throughout history, humans have been fascinated by the continuous march of time. As various events unfold in this temporal continuum, they produce measurable sequences indicative of their evolution. This leads us to the concept of a "time series."

A time series is a set of data points arranged in chronological order. These points are typically captured at consistent intervals, although there are exceptions. Examples abound daily stock market closings, temperature readings taken every hour, or annual population counts. One of the defining characteristics of time series data is its emphasis on the time dimension. While other datasets might focus on spatial or categorical attributes, time series data prioritizes the sequential arrangement of values.

Some defining features of time series data include:

Trend: Over long stretches, a time series can exhibit a consistent trajectory, be it upward, downward, or more nuanced. An example might be the steady rise in global temperatures over several decades.

Seasonality: Patterns that repeat at known intervals characterize many time series. Examples include retail sales spikes during holiday seasons or predictable daily traffic jams.

Cyclic Movements: Different from seasonality, cyclic movements lack a fixed duration. The economic cycles of growth and recession serve as an example.

Random Variations: In addition to regular patterns, there are unforeseen fluctuations in time series data, resulting from unpredictable events or anomalies.

Time series data is valuable for several reasons:

Predictive Analysis: One primary use of time series analysis is forecasting. Businesses leverage it to anticipate sales, stock requirements, or consumer demand.

Historical Insights: Visual representations of time series data can unveil patterns or trends that might have been overlooked.

Event Impact Assessment: Time series allows for evaluating the influence of specific events. A company might utilize it to measure the efficacy of an advertising campaign.

Cause-effect Relationships: Sometimes, the goal might be to check if one time series can predict another beyond mere correlation.

However, analyzing time series data isn't without its challenges. Autocorrelation, a scenario where data points in the series influence one another, is commonly observed. Additionally, non-stationarity, where the dataset's statistical attributes change over time, can pose analytical hurdles.

Today's technological landscape offers a wide array of methods to tackle time series data, from traditional models like ARIMA to cutting-edge techniques involving neural networks and LSTM models.

In essence, time series serves as a structured record of events as they unfold over time. Whether the task at hand is predicting stock market trends, gauging public opinion dynamics, or tracking climate variations, time series data remains invaluable. With the growth of data science and machine learning, the significance and versatility of time series analysis are poised to reach new heights, providing deeper insights into patterns woven through time.

Techniques for time series forecasting

Time series forecasting is an essential analytical tool used in a variety of fields, from financial markets and economics to weather forecasting and healthcare. By examining historical data, it aims to predict future trends. Here, we will delve into some key techniques employed in this field over time.

Simple Moving Average (SMA):

Essentially, SMA forecasts the future by looking at the mean of past values within a chosen timeframe. However, it might not be the best fit for data exhibiting strong trends or cyclic patterns.

Exponential Smoothing (ES):

In this method, older observations are given decreasing importance, whereas recent ones are given more significance. Single Exponential Smoothing suits data without evident trends, while Double and Triple Exponential Smoothing can capture both trends and seasonality.

Autoregressive Integrated Moving Average (ARIMA):

Blending the autoregressive (AR) and moving average (MA) strategies, ARIMA stands as a cornerstone for time series predictions. It incorporates differencing, making it apt for non-stationary data. For seasonal data, Seasonal ARIMA (SARIMA) is preferred.

Prophet:

Crafted by the research unit at Facebook, Prophet specializes in handling datasets exhibiting multiple seasonal variations. It's especially potent for data with anomalies, missing values, or unexpected trend alterations.

State Space Models and Kalman Filtering:

This dynamic technique views time series as transitioning through various states. The Kalman Filter, a core component, iteratively refines state estimates, leading to accurate forecasts.

Long Short-Term Memory Networks (LSTM):

Belonging to the Recurrent Neural Network (RNN) family, LSTM excels in sequence predictions. Designed to manage extended data dependencies, it's now a popular choice for intricate forecasting endeavors.

Proximity-Based Models:

Approaches like the k-Nearest Neighbors (k-NN) are modified for time series, making predictions based on how patterns have historically evolved.

Vector AutoRegressive Models (VAR):

When dealing with multiple interconnected variables in a time-dependent setting, VAR becomes invaluable. It concurrently models the interplay between numerous series.

Hybrid Models:

In some scenarios, a combination of models, like meshing ARIMA with neural networks, can lead to more precise predictions.

Decomposition Methods:

These techniques, such as STL (Seasonal and Trend decomposition using Loess), segment time series data into trend, seasonality, and residual parts, allowing for separate modeling and consequent combination.

Bayesian Structural Time Series (BSTS):

Merging state space models with Bayesian techniques, BSTS can incorporate external data, optimizing adaptability and efficiency.

To select the most suitable forecasting method, a thorough preliminary analysis of the data is imperative. Factors like seasonality, existing trends, and potential outliers play a role in this choice.

Moreover, validating the chosen model is crucial. Techniques such as walk-forward validation or time series cross-validation help in fine-tuning the model. Advanced methods also necessitate substantial computational prowess and a deep understanding of related tools.

In conclusion, the art and science of time series forecasting seamlessly integrate traditional methods with cutting-edge algorithms. As our digital age produces more data, the quest for refined forecasting methods will continue, meeting the diverse needs of both industry and academia.

Application in financial, retail, and other sectors

The unfolding digital age emphasizes the necessity of insights derived from data for industries aiming to streamline operations, boost customer engagement, and carve out a niche in the market. The utilization of data science transcends various sectors, with particular emphasis on its transformative impact in finance and retail. However, its influence isn't confined to these sectors alone. Its ripple effect is evident in fields as varied as healthcare and energy optimization. Let's examine the multifaceted roles of data science across these sectors.

Financial Domain:

Within the intricate world of finance, with its myriad transactions and evolving market dynamics, data science becomes indispensable in:

Automated Trading: Sophisticated algorithms enable traders to make swift transactions, capturing profit from the slightest market variations.

Identifying Fraud: By processing vast transactional histories, machine learning models are equipped to recognize and alert unusual patterns, acting as a first line of defense against potential fraud.

Evaluating Credit: Beyond traditional methods, the vast amount of data now available allows financial entities to gauge an individual's financial reliability using a broader spectrum of data, including online interactions.

Strategic Risk Mitigation: Predictive tools empower institutions to forecast market trends, enabling pre-emptive strategies to navigate potential economic fluctuations.

Retail Domain:

The retail landscape, propelled by e-commerce, is underpinned by data-driven strategies.

Tailored Marketing: Data insights allow retailers to customize product suggestions and ads, amplifying the potential for increased sales.

Efficient Supply Chain Management: By predicting demand, retailers can maintain optimal inventory, minimize overhead costs, and avoid stock-outs.

Dynamic Pricing: Advanced pricing algorithms adapt in real-time, taking into account various factors to optimize profit margins.

Assessing Customer Feedback: By scanning and analyzing online feedback and social interactions, businesses can adapt to align better with market sentiment.

Healthcare Sector:

Healthcare, a cornerstone of any society, stands to gain significantly from data science.

Proactive Healthcare: Algorithms can assess patient histories and indicate potential health risks, ensuring early intervention.

Advanced Imaging: Techniques like Convolutional Neural Networks (CNNs) have revolutionized diagnostic accuracy in medical imaging, sometimes surpassing human experts.

Accelerated Drug Development: The conventional drug creation route is lengthy and expensive. Data analytics can identify potential drug interactions faster, making the development process more efficient.

Energy Domain:

As the focus shifts towards sustainable resources, the role of data science becomes pivotal.

Consumption Predictions: Analytical models can forecast energy usage patterns, leading to more strategic resource distribution.

Proactive Infrastructure Upkeep: Real-time data from embedded sensors can predict equipment failures, enabling timely maintenance.

Transport Sector:

From public conveyance to cargo logistics, transportation has been transformed by data science.

Optimizing Routes: For efficient deliveries, logistics entities deploy algorithms to determine ideal paths, considering factors like traffic and fuel efficiency.

Ridership Analysis: By assessing usage patterns, public transport entities can fine-tune schedules to cater to peak demand times.

In sum, the influence of data science has permeated diverse industries, facilitating operational efficacy, cost-effectiveness, and heightened service quality. With technological evolution showing no signs of slowing down, the deepening interplay between industries and data science promises a future steered by informed decisions.

Chapter Ten

Big Data and Data Engineering

What is big data?

Big Data, a term that has permeated the technical and business realms, seems relatively straightforward at face value. It denotes large datasets that appear unwieldy. However, the real essence of Big Data is not just its magnitude but the implications and prospects it presents across myriad sectors, from technological innovations to business strategies and societal shifts.

Fundamentally, Big Data encapsulates datasets that are immense, diverse, and evolving too rapidly for conventional data management tools to handle. Yet, its true essence lies in the capability to process, analyze, and extract actionable insights from such extensive collections. To delve deeper into the world of Big Data, several key facets emerge:

1. Key Characteristics of Big Data – The Three Vs:

Big Data's traditional definition hinges on three pivotal attributes, colloquially termed the "3Vs":

Volume: Pertains to the enormous size of the data, scaling from terabytes to exabytes and more. The surge in digital devices and platforms contributes to an ever-expanding data landscape.

Velocity: Refers to the rapid rate at which data is produced and gathered. Examples include millisecond-by-millisecond stock trades or the incessant influx of social media content.

Variety: Highlights the diverse data types, encompassing structured forms like databases, unstructured ones like textual content, or semi-structured formats such as XML or JSON. The spectrum of data sources, from embedded sensors to online platforms, has never been more extensive.

While the 3Vs form the bedrock, additional characteristics, such as Veracity (the reliability of data) and Value (data's potential utility), enrich the understanding of Big Data.

2. Origins and Production:

The digital era's dawn, with its vast array of devices, platforms, and sensors, has catalyzed a remarkable data generation rate. Notable contributors include:

IoT Devices: Devices spanning from personal health monitors to industrial equipment relay continuous streams of data.

Social Media: Digital footprints, spanning likes, shares, and posts, chronicle user interactions and inclinations.

E-Commerce Platforms: Beyond transactional data, these platforms record user behaviors, interests, and browsing histories.

Governmental and Organizational Records: Immense datasets encompassing population demographics, civic amenities, and more are maintained by institutions.

3. Analytical Challenges and Potential:

Simply amassing data reserves is insufficient. The crux lies in harnessing its potential, necessitating sophisticated analytical tools. Key challenges entail:

Storage: Storing vast data necessitates evolving storage solutions, often gravitating towards systems like Hadoop.

Processing: Conventional software falls short in addressing Big Data's demands, necessitating cutting-edge, frequently real-time, solutions.

Analysis: Applying intricate statistical or machine learning models on such datasets requires robust computational prowess.

Maintaining Data Quality: Ensuring consistency, quality, and reliability becomes exponentially challenging with data growth.

Yet, navigating these challenges unlocks unparalleled opportunities. Comprehensive Big Data analysis can illuminate market trajectories, operational optimizations, and untapped revenue avenues.

4. Sector-wide Repercussions:

Big Data's potential ripples across diverse sectors:

Healthcare: Big Data's applications range from bespoke patient care using predictive models to expansive genetic research projects.

Finance: Sectors like high-frequency trading, anti-fraud measures, and tailored customer outreach leverage Big Data.

Retail: Through Big Data, businesses can anticipate market movements, streamline supply logistics, and curate personalized customer journeys.

Urban Development: In the realm of urbanization, Big Data aids in infrastructural planning, optimizing energy consumption, and refining traffic management.

In summation, Big Data transcends mere data collection. It signifies a transformative approach to how businesses harness, interpret, and deploy information. As our technological arsenal continues to expand, Big Data's boundaries will be determined by our visionary ambitions and our capacity to derive profound insights.

Tools and technologies like Hadoop and Spark

In today's data-centric world, efficient tools and platforms are paramount for handling, analyzing, and gleaning insights from massive data sets. Within this context, Hadoop and Spark stand as frontrunners, ushering in a new era of data processing and management. To grasp their essence, it's beneficial to explore their structures, potential, and what sets them apart.

Hadoop: The Foundation of Big Data Processing

Hadoop, an initiative by the Apache Software Foundation, is a pioneering framework tailored for distributed data processing. Its reputation as a linchpin in big data hinges on two integral components:

Hadoop Distributed File System (HDFS): An ingenious storage solution, HDFS segments extensive data files into manageable blocks, spreading them over multiple machines in a network. Its replication strategy guarantees data durability, with each block saved on several nodes.

MapReduce: The crux of Hadoop's processing mechanism, MapReduce is a paradigm for parallel data treatment. It distributes tasks into smaller units, executed simultaneously across the network. Conceptually, the 'Map' phase categorizes data into key-value structures, while the 'Reduce' phase subsequently aggregates and interprets these pairs.

Apache Spark: Setting the Pace with In-Memory Computing

Apache Spark has carved its niche as an advanced data processing platform, building on the legacy of Hadoop but adding flair with its in-memory computations. This methodology considerably reduces operations reliant on disk storage. Spark's core pillars encompass:

Resilient Distributed Dataset (RDD): An immutable, distributed array of items, RDD is Spark's foundational data construct, imbued with features to recover from unexpected node disruptions.

Spark SQL: An interface for structured data interrogation, it offers a platform to deploy SQL-esque queries on datasets.

MLlib: An expansive library for machine learning tasks, facilitating diverse operations from clustering to regression.

GraphX: A dedicated computation library for graph-based data, allowing a dual view of datasets—as graphs and collections.

Spark Streaming: A conduit for real-time data processing, invaluable for scenarios necessitating on-the-fly insights.

Contrasting Hadoop and Spark

A side-by-side evaluation illuminates their individual strengths:

Operational Speed: With its in-memory model, Spark often outpaces Hadoop's MapReduce, which leans on disk-based operations.

User Experience: Spark's developer-friendly APIs simplify its adoption, whereas Hadoop's MapReduce can be intricate and demands deeper familiarity.

Reliability: Hadoop's HDFS provides resilience via data block replication. Similarly, Spark's RDD can regenerate data after unforeseen disruptions.

Functionality Scope: Spark offers a more comprehensive toolkit, adept at handling batch, real-time, machine learning, and graph-based tasks. In contrast, Hadoop's MapReduce mainly focuses on batch operations.

Investment: Spark's penchant for in-memory operations can be pricier due to higher RAM requirements, but it compensates with performance dividends.

Synergy: Hadoop and Spark can coexist harmoniously. Spark often taps into HDFS for storage needs, merging their strengths.

Wrap-Up

Hadoop and Spark, with their unique offerings, have substantially influenced the trajectory of big data. Hadoop, with its resilience and economical storage solutions, is apt for massive data storage. On the other hand, Spark, with its speed and adaptability, fits seamlessly into real-time analytics.

The continued evolution and interplay of these technologies will undoubtedly dictate the future roadmap of big data exploration and its endless possibilities.

Data pipelines and architectures

In the evolving digital ecosystem, data is the linchpin that drives actionable insights and strategic decisions. For a smooth, efficient flow of data from its origin to its point of utility, a strong infrastructure is paramount. This brings us to the significance of data pipelines and architectures, which are instrumental in converting raw data into meaningful information.

Navigating Data Pipelines

A data pipeline is a sequence of processes that guide and modify data as it journeys from its source to its endpoint. Think of it as a conduit through which data, much like liquid through a tube, passes from beginning to end, getting refined along the way.

The Anatomy of a Data Pipeline:

Acquisition: The phase where data from various origins, including databases, live streams, and logs, is accumulated.

Modification: Here, data undergoes alterations—purification, augmentation, and organization to align with end-user requirements.

Conservation: The phase where refined data finds a home in structured storage spaces like data lakes or warehouses.

Interpretation: This phase utilizes analytical tools to extract value from the stored data.

Representation: This final step converts analytical results into user-friendly formats, simplifying decision processes.

Pipeline Varieties:

Batch Operations: This kind processes data in predetermined chunks, ideal for handling large quantities without immediacy.

Instantaneous Operations: As the name suggests, this processes data as it emerges, catering to applications where time is of the essence.

Blended: A versatile mix of batch and real-time processes.

Structuring with Data Architecture

Data architecture is a blueprint that charts the life cycle of data, right from its acquisition to its deployment across a business. It ensures that data remains accessible, trustworthy, and protected.

Key Elements:

Data Schematics: Detailed layouts that prescribe how data should be stored, arranged, and retrieved, ensuring uniformity.

Storage Solutions: While everyday data is maintained in databases, data warehouses are repositories that store a mix of structured and unstructured data for deeper analysis.

Data Synchronization: This process ensures that data from various origins seamlessly blend, offering a cohesive perspective.

Data Stewardship: Protocols that govern the data's usability, integrity, and safeguarding.

Design Patterns:

Unified: A traditional approach where all data facets are interwoven and interdependent, ideal for static settings.

Modular Services: This style divides functions into small, autonomous units that interact via standardized communication channels, ideal for scalability.

Event-responsive: A design that pivots around immediate events and their subsequent actions, apt for dynamic, real-time scenarios.

The Symbiotic Relationship

The partnership between data pipelines and architecture is pivotal. The architecture lays out the plan, and the pipelines act as the channels that actualize this plan. Together, they ensure:

Scale: Adapts to increasing data volumes and diverse speeds.

Versatility: Manages an array of data kinds and origins.

Durability: Guarantees consistent data access and recovery mechanisms.

Efficiency: Streamlines data movement, cutting down on delays and impediments.

The Horizon Ahead:

The demand for data-centric solutions is propelling transformative changes in both data pipelines and architectures:

AI-Optimized Pipelines: Incorporates artificial intelligence to enhance data transition, pinpoint irregularities, and self-rectify hitches.

Diversified Cloud Architectures: Distributes data resources across multiple cloud platforms, boosting uptime and disaster recuperation.

Agile Data Management: Infuses adaptive methodologies into data handling, promoting swift innovation and reducing the data-to-insight cycle.

In Summary

The world of data pipelines and architectures goes beyond mere data management—it's about harnessing potential. As data becomes more pervasive, these frameworks will be the pillars ensuring ethical, efficient, and purposeful use of data.

They are set to become even more intricate and pivotal, forming the backbone of a data-driven world.

Chapter Eleven

Data Visualization Techniques

Importance of data visualization

In an era dominated by digital data, the real obstacle often isn't in its accumulation but in deciphering its meaning. Data visualization elegantly merges artistic representation with scientific precision, offering a bridge between dense data clusters and intuitive human understanding. By offering a graphic representation of data, it unveils underlying trends, anomalies, and patterns that might remain concealed within tables of unprocessed data.

Why Visualization Matters

Humans are naturally predisposed to process visual information more efficiently than text or numbers. Research from the Massachusetts Institute of Technology indicates that our brains can recognize visual elements in an astonishing 13 milliseconds. Hence, a well-designed chart or diagram can narrate a comprehensive story much more effectively than rows of figures on a spreadsheet.

Perks of Data Visualization

Swift Interpretation: Visualizing data through charts or graphs facilitates instant comprehension. In industries where decisions are time-bound, this speed is invaluable.

Spotting Trends: Patterns and correlations surface more readily through visual representation. For businesses, visualizing sales data might uncover seasonality, guiding subsequent marketing initiatives.

Unearthing Issues: Visualization simplifies the task of spotting anomalies. Whether it's a sudden drop in website visitors or an unexpected surge in product returns, visual aids make problem detection straightforward.

Narrating with Data: A narrative rooted in data holds potent persuasive capabilities. Through visualization, these narratives gain vivacity, making discussions more engaging.

Better Recall: Visual elements reinforce memory. During strategy deliberations, participants are more likely to remember visualized data than mere numbers.

The Diverse Applications of Data Visualization

Steering Decisions: Executive meetings, where organizational futures are molded, greatly benefit from data visualization. These tools provide a clear picture of current trends, prospective outlooks, and potential scenarios, ensuring leadership is well-informed.

Supporting Research: In scholarly circles, complex research findings can be condensed and portrayed visually, simplifying intricate topics and underscoring the research's relevance.

Public Insight: Civic bodies and institutions can leverage visualization to inform the masses about pertinent issues, from health metrics to fiscal patterns, making the data both relatable and easy to grasp.

Potential Pitfalls

Though data visualization has undeniable benefits, it's crucial to recognize potential missteps. Misapplied, it can confuse rather than clarify:

Misleading Scales: The narrative of a graph can be altered significantly by tweaking its scales. Consistent and transparent scales are vital.

Excessive Simplification: Striving for simplicity is good, but overdoing it can strip the data of crucial details.

Lacking Context: Data requires context for relevance. Visualization should always encapsulate the broader story for comprehensive understanding.

Looking Forward

With the constant surge in data volume and intricacy, the role of visualization will only intensify. Future visualizations, leveraging technologies like augmented reality (AR) and virtual reality (VR), promise a more engaging, immersive experience.

Emerging tools and platforms, harnessing the power of artificial intelligence and machine learning, are set to introduce predictive visualization techniques, granting users the ability to project future scenarios based on historical data.

In Summary

Data visualization has transitioned from being a mere embellishment to an absolute necessity in the modern data-centric world. It serves as the magnifying glass, zooming into vast datasets to extract comprehensible, actionable insights. As entities worldwide grapple with data's increasing significance, visualization emerges as the beacon, guiding them toward informed strategies and insightful decision-making.

Tools for data visualization e.g., Matplotlib, Seaborn, Tableau

In today's data-rich environment, the ability to articulate data in an understandable format is crucial. Data visualization tools, like Matplotlib, Seaborn, and Tableau, have emerged as pivotal players, aiding professionals in presenting data in a coherent and engaging manner. Each tool possesses its individual merits and specializes in different aspects of the visualization domain.

Matplotlib: Python's Visualization Pioneer

Background and Scope:

Born from a need to replicate MATLAB's capabilities within Python, Matplotlib has grown into a primary choice for Python enthusiasts since its inception by John Hunter in 2003. Recognized for its adaptability, Matplotlib allows users to create a plethora of plots, suitable for various platforms.

Prominent Features:

Diversity: Ranging from bar graphs to intricate 3D visuals, Matplotlib caters to a wide audience.

Tailoring Abilities: Users have significant control over their visual designs, ensuring each graph's uniqueness.

Python Synchronization: Its compatibility with Python-based applications amplifies its desirability among developers.

Drawbacks to Consider:

The expansive nature of Matplotlib can be daunting for beginners, and the journey to mastery may seem elongated for some.

Seaborn: Python's Answer to Statistical Graphics

Background and Scope:

An offshoot of Matplotlib, Seaborn brings a fresh perspective, focusing on providing an elevated interface for statistical visuals. It's the go-to tool for those aiming to craft aesthetic and informative statistical representations.

Prominent Features:

Data Integration: Designed to work harmoniously with Pandas DataFrames, Seaborn makes data visualization a breeze.

Aesthetic Themes: Out-of-the-box themes are available to enhance the beauty of Matplotlib's outputs.

Complex Visuals Simplified: Seaborn effortlessly produces advanced statistical graphs.

Drawbacks to Consider:

For those seeking a wider variety of non-statistical plots, Seaborn might seem somewhat restrictive.

Tableau: A Foray into Interactive Visualization

Background and Scope:

Differing from Python libraries, Tableau is a dedicated software tailored for crafting interactive and dynamic data visuals. With its stronghold in the business intelligence sector, Tableau transforms intricate data sets into easily digestible visual stories.

Prominent Features:

User-Friendly Design: Tableau's intuitive drag-and-drop feature welcomes both coders and non-coders.

Engaging Dashboards: Beyond static visuals, Tableau offers a realm of interactive exploration.

Extensive Compatibility: From local databases to cloud infrastructures, Tableau ensures seamless data connections.

Drawbacks to Consider:

While feature-rich, Tableau comes with a price tag. Moreover, for specific data preprocessing tasks, other platforms might be more suitable.

Making the Informed Choice: Context Matters

The decision between Matplotlib, Seaborn, and Tableau should align with individual needs and scenarios:

Those well-versed in Python and desiring meticulous control over design elements will resonate with Matplotlib.

When the objective revolves around creating stellar statistical plots in Python, Seaborn becomes an evident choice.

In business settings where engaging, code-free, and interactive visual stories are paramount, Tableau is unparalleled.

Concluding Thoughts

As we navigate the vast world of data visualization, tools like Matplotlib, Seaborn, and Tableau serve as guiding lights. Each, with its distinct offerings, paves the way to visual storytelling. Familiarizing oneself with their core competencies is the cornerstone to leveraging their capabilities, leading to enriched and captivating data narratives.

Best practices

In today's rapidly evolving professional environment, the key to success lies not just in possessing expertise or resources, but in how one applies them. This brings us to the concept of best practices, which are established procedures or systems identified through extensive research and experience. Adopting these practices ensures optimal outcomes by mitigating common mistakes and optimizing proven strategies.

Origins of Best Practices

The foundation of best practices stems from examining repeated challenges and pinpointing the most effective solutions to them. As certain methodologies demonstrate superior results over others, they emerge as benchmarks for future endeavors. Disseminating these benchmarks broadens the scope for efficiency and reduces the likelihood of mistakes.

Characteristics of Best Practices

Effectiveness and Resource Utilization: Best practices pave the way for desired outcomes while ensuring resource allocation is maximized, harmonizing results with resource consumption.

Consistency: A hallmark of best practices is their ability to yield steady results across diverse settings. Their standardized nature guarantees predictable outputs when implemented aptly.

Adaptability: While they provide a well-defined route, best practices are not set in stone. Their inherent flexibility allows customization to fit distinct circumstances.

Domain-Specific Applications

Best practices have found their way into multiple professional arenas, each with its specific set of standardized methodologies:

Software Creation: From the adoption of agile techniques to thorough code evaluations and comprehensive testing, best practices ensure the development of reliable and user-centric software.

Project Execution: Employing tools like Gantt charts, comprehensive risk evaluations, and clear communication channels guarantees the seamless progression of projects.

Data Handling: Practices focusing on data consistency, robust security measures, and validation checks are imperative to maintain data accuracy and safety.

Production: Approaches like Lean manufacturing processes, Six Sigma, and holistic quality management concentrate on waste reduction and quality enhancement.

Potential Pitfalls and Aspects to Ponder

While best practices present numerous advantages, it's vital to be wary of potential drawbacks:

Excessive Dependence: Relying solely on existing best practices can limit novel solutions. They should act as guides rather than strict mandates.

Lack of Contextual Awareness: Blindly applying a best practice without comprehending its relevance can be counterproductive. It's paramount to discern its applicability in a given situation.

Evolutionary Dynamics: In sectors that undergo rapid changes, today's best practices might be tomorrow's outdated methods. Keeping abreast of updates is crucial.

Navigating the Future

For those looking to lead in their fields, embracing best practices is just the beginning. Enhancing their journey involves:

Ongoing Education: Keeping oneself updated with sector-specific advancements ensures that practices remain relevant.

Incorporating Feedback: Actively seeking and integrating critiques can foster growth and refinement.

Tailoring Practices: Modify established practices to meet the unique needs of varied tasks.

Recording and Dissemination: Upon devising an effective new approach, chronicling and sharing it can elevate the collective knowledge base.

Wrapping Up

Best practices act as guiding beacons, illuminating the path to excellence by leveraging accumulated wisdom. By assimilating, refining, and sharing these practices, professionals can not only optimize their endeavors but also enhance the overarching standards of their domain.

Chapter Twelve

Ethics in Data Science

Data privacy and security

The digital era is characterized by data's omnipresence. Ranging from personal details to transaction logs, this data wields immense influence. However, the great potential of data is matched by an equal measure of accountability. Hence, the intertwined concepts of data privacy and security have come to the fore. This piece sheds light on these realms, underscoring their importance and offering insights into their comprehensive application.

Data Privacy: Championing Individual Autonomy

Data privacy is all about the ethical management, processing, and usage of data, keeping the rights of the individual paramount. At its core, data privacy aims to ensure that individual-related data remains both confidential and untouched without clear and well-informed consent.

Principal Elements of Data Privacy:

User Autonomy: Individuals must be the true owners of their data. They should be duly notified about its acquisition and possess the autonomy to give or withhold consent.

Usage Restrictions: Data should be leveraged solely for the intentions declared during its gathering, precluding any unforeseen exploitations.

Data Accessibility: Individuals must have avenues to retrieve their data, rectify inconsistencies, and even advocate its removal under particular conditions.

Data Security: The Digital Bulwark

While privacy outlines rights and choices, security is all about measures to shield data from unsolicited access, theft, and breaches. This combines a medley of regulations, methodologies, and technological safeguards aimed at defending data from both internal and external menaces.

Essential Facets of Data Security

Tangible Protections: This pertains to physical measures like fortified data storage sites, access controls through biometrics, constant monitoring, and provisions for data recovery.

Securing Network Pathways: Implementing tools such as encrypted barriers, systems to detect trespassers, and security protocols to fend off unwarranted digital intrusions.

Safeguarding Applications: This zeroes in on fortifying specific software applications through means like timely updates, code assessments, and rigorous vulnerability tests.

The Symbiosis of Privacy and Security

Having security without privacy is conceivable, but the inverse—privacy without security—is unviable. For instance, an entity might fortify its data against external intrusions but could exploit it internally, thereby flouting privacy norms. Hence, robust security is foundational for meaningful privacy.

Global Regulatory Landscapes

The global acknowledgment of these facets has spurred legislative actions. One standout example is the European Union's General Data Protection Regulation (GDPR), which mandates rigorous privacy and security standards, placing individuals' rights at center stage. This global movement has seen many countries enact comparable regulations, underlining the universal significance of the issues at hand.

Navigating the Challenges

The journey towards comprehensive privacy and security isn't without its obstacles:

The Dynamic Nature of Threats: The continuous evolution of technology results in equally evolving cyber threats, calling for persistent alertness and adaptive counter-strategies.

Harmonizing Access with Security: A perennial challenge is ensuring data is both secure and accessible for legitimate pursuits.

Diverse Regulatory Mandates: International enterprises grapple with diverse, and at times, contradictory regulatory landscapes across regions.

Chartering a Future with Data Integrity

To traverse the intricate maze of data privacy and security, a diversified approach is required:

Unified Approach: Fostering an organizational ethos that gives precedence to data safety, embracing technology, processes, and human-centric solutions.

Continuous Adaptation: In this rapidly transforming digital space, ongoing education, and flexibility hold the key. Periodic upskilling sessions and safety exercises can keep an organization in a state of readiness.

Open Dialogue: Open channels of communication about data handling practices can cultivate stakeholder trust. Being transparent, especially during data breaches, along with immediate corrective measures, can mitigate potential repercussions.

Synergistic Alliances: Addressing sophisticated challenges often demands collaborative initiatives. Allying with cybersecurity agencies, active participation in security alliances, and pooling intelligence can enhance defensive competencies.

Final Reflections

As our digital interactions deepen, the twin principles of data privacy and security take on added significance. Striking the right balance between safeguarding individual freedoms and ensuring data integrity will shape the trust landscape of our digital interactions. Through informed tactics and a proactive stance, we can navigate toward a digital landscape where data serves as an enabler, not a liability.

Bias and fairness

In an era dominated by data, we increasingly depend on algorithms to inform decisions that touch numerous areas of our daily lives, from mortgage approvals to health diagnoses. Given this growing reliance, issues of bias and fairness have emerged as critical considerations. This analysis aims to explore these concerns, highlighting the inherent challenges and proposing potential solutions within the broader context of computational ethics.

Unraveling the Complexity of Algorithmic Bias

In the world of algorithms, bias represents systematic and unwarranted disparities toward certain groups based on specific traits. Various factors can inadvertently introduce bias into models:

Past Data: Algorithms trained on historical datasets laden with existing biases can perpetuate those very prejudices.

Imbalanced Sampling: A dataset that doesn't adequately represent the wider population can produce biased conclusions. For instance, if a health dataset is disproportionately skewed toward one gender, the results might not be as reliable for the other.

Feature Choices: Selecting the wrong input features can result in bias, particularly if these features have ties to sensitive attributes like ethnicity or gender.

Defining Fairness: More Than One Dimension

Fairness isn't a one-size-fits-all concept; its meaning shifts based on context and the viewpoints of stakeholders. Key fairness concepts include:

Demographic Equality: This is achieved if the decisions made by a model are unaffected by protected attributes.

Balanced Outcomes: This ensures that algorithms have similar rates of true positives and false positives across all demographic segments.

Individual Justice: This emphasizes that individuals with comparable profiles should receive similar outcomes, underscoring the significance of context.

Obstacles in Counteracting Bias and Promoting Fairness

Pinpointing Fairness: Given its multiple interpretations, deciding on the most suitable definition of fairness for a specific task can be a conundrum.

Navigating Trade-offs: Pursuing fairness might sometimes mean compromising model precision. Deciding on the right balance demands careful consideration.

Deep-Seated Biases: Some areas have long-standing biases, which makes it challenging to identify and neutralize the skewed elements.

Strategies for Ethical Algorithmic Decisions

An all-encompassing strategy, blending proactive and reactive measures, is essential for more unbiased systems:

Holistic Data Gathering: Making sure datasets are thorough and representative can lower the chances of biased results. Diverse teams in data gathering can further amplify this effect.

Interventions to Foster Fairness: Techniques specially designed to improve model fairness can be employed. Methods like regularization, adversarial approaches, and reweighting stand out.

Routine Bias Checks: Frequent checks to spot and correct biases can bolster model resilience. Tools like Fairness Indicators or AI Fairness 360 can be handy for such reviews.

Open Reporting: Offering clear insights into model outcomes, particularly regarding fairness metrics, can build trust and allow external evaluations.

Cross-Disciplinary Cooperation: Engaging professionals from fields like ethics, sociology, and specific industries can offer valuable perspectives on fairness.

Incorporating Stakeholder Views: Engaging those directly affected by decisions can provide more comprehensive and accepted definitions of fairness.

Expanding the Ethical Horizon Beyond Bias and Fairness

Though paramount, bias and fairness are just two elements in the vast ethical AI arena. Other crucial aspects like transparency, responsibility, and data privacy should also be at the forefront. Thus, a thorough approach to ethical AI must be all-encompassing, integrating all these elements.

To Conclude

In a future steered by algorithms, the ethical consequences of these systems become central to our discourse. Tackling issues of bias and fairness, albeit intricate, remains fundamental. Solutions might lie at the intersection of technological advancements, ethical considerations, and human discernment. Ensuring that algorithms uphold values of inclusivity and justice is more than just a technical challenge—

it's a societal mandate that will shape our collective digital journey.

Responsible AI and ML

The rapid advances in artificial intelligence (AI) and machine learning (ML) have ushered in unprecedented capabilities, but with these come significant ethical and practical considerations. The term "Responsible AI and ML" encompasses the principles and practices ensuring that these technologies are developed and applied with a sense of duty, moral integrity, and for the benefit of all.

Foundational Principles of Ethical AI and ML

1. Equitability: The data sets used to train AI and ML models might contain inherent biases. It's essential to regularly scrutinize and adjust these models to prevent the unintended perpetuation of these biases, ensuring a level playing field for all demographics.

2. Responsibility: It's crucial to establish clear lines of responsibility when it comes to the creation and deployment of AI systems. Firms must have procedures in place to address and rectify any AI-related mishaps or misapplications.

3. Clarity: The intricate nature of certain AI mechanisms, notably in deep learning, can obfuscate their decision-making processes. A move towards clarity means creating models where their decision-making rationales can be deciphered and justified.

4. Data Integrity: Data is pivotal for AI's functioning. It's of utmost importance that the procurement, storage, and utilization of this data prioritize and respect individual privacy rights. Methods like differential privacy present solutions that allow models to draw insights without compromising individual data.

Barriers to Ethical AI Implementation

1. Varied Perspectives: Ethical benchmarks might vary across different cultures and communities. Setting universally acknowledged standards poses a challenge.

2. Technological Constraints: Despite the emphasis on clear AI, some of the most potent models are often those that are not easily understandable.

3. Market Dynamics: The race to remain at the forefront technologically can sometimes overshadow the significance of ethical deployment, resulting in premature roll-outs.

Strategies for Ethical AI Adoption

1. Cross-functional Partnerships: Collaborating with specialists from varied fields—like ethics, psychology, or sociology—can lead to a holistic understanding of AI's broader ramifications.

2. Ethical Frameworks: Drafting comprehensive guidelines or codes that govern AI development can serve as a touchstone for developers and organizations.

3. Prioritizing Research: Breaking barriers such as the balance between model transparency and efficiency necessitates dedicated research in domains like explainable AI.

4. Ongoing Oversight: Post-deployment, AI models should be under persistent observation to ensure they maintain their integrity and fairness as they interact with evolving real-world data.

5. Engaging the Public: Gathering insights from the broader community and users can shed light on potential blind spots and areas of contention.

Global Efforts Toward Ethical AI

Globally, the gravity of responsible AI has been acknowledged. From industry leaders to regulatory bodies, there's a concerted effort to draft and adopt ethical AI principles. Prominent examples include Google's AI Principles, underscore safety, fairness, and clarity, and the EU's guidelines advocating transparency and societal welfare.

Responsibility in AI: An Ever-evolving Commitment

Attaining responsible AI is a journey with no fixed end. As the domain of AI and ML morphs, so will the associated ethical considerations. An ongoing exchange of ideas among developers, regulators, and the general public is fundamental to ensuring that AI serves both its primary functions and the broader societal values.

Concluding Thoughts

The strides made in AI and ML are transformative. As these tools become ingrained in our societal fabric, their ethical deployment becomes increasingly paramount. By adhering to principles like equitability, responsibility, clarity, and data integrity, and by proactively tackling inherent challenges, we're laying the groundwork for an era where AI amplifies human potential while reflecting our collective ethics and aspirations.

Chapter Thirteen

Advanced Data Science Tools and Frameworks

Overview of tools like TensorFlow, Scikit-learn, and Keras

In the vibrant landscape of machine learning and deep learning platforms, several tools have emerged as leaders due to their robust capabilities and wide acceptance. Among them, TensorFlow, Scikit-learn, and Keras hold prime positions. Let's unpack a brief exploration of each and highlight their main features.

1. TensorFlow

Background and Structure

Spawned from the labs of the Google Brain team, TensorFlow is an open-source platform primarily recognized for deep learning applications. It's designed for distributed computing, making it compatible with various devices from single computers to vast server clusters.

Distinct Features

Tensors as Building Blocks: At its core, TensorFlow revolves around tensors, which are multi-dimensional data arrays ideal for a variety of data types.

Graph-based Computation: The tool works by creating a computational graph. Each node in this graph stands for operations, while the connecting edges symbolize tensors in transit.

Versatility: Whether it's a single CPU, multiple GPUs, or even mobile devices, TensorFlow is adaptable, making it a cornerstone for expansive machine learning operations.

Variants: The platform has diversified to accommodate TensorFlow Lite (for lightweight devices) and TensorFlow.js (suitable for web-based deployments).

2. Scikit-learn

Background and Structure

Built on stalwarts like NumPy and SciPy, Scikit-learn is a Python-focused machine learning library, steering more towards classic machine learning methods rather than deep learning.

Distinct Features

Comprehensive Algorithm Suite: Scikit-learn brings to the fore a vast array of algorithms, from supervised tasks like regression to unsupervised ones such as clustering.

Pipeline Formulation: The library introduces a mechanism to create computational sequences, streamlining multiple steps into a cohesive flow.

Efficient Model Assessment: Equipped with numerous tools for gauging model performance, Scikit-learn simplifies processes like metrics calculation and parameter tuning.

Ready-to-use Data Tools: Scikit-learn incorporates tools for essential data modifications like scaling, encoding, and filling gaps, prepping data for machine learning models.

3. Keras

Background and Structure

Starting as a frontend for Theano, Keras transitioned into an independent deep learning tool, primarily aligning with TensorFlow as its backend.

Distinct Features

Simplified Interface: By abstracting intricate details, Keras makes it seamless for developers to craft neural networks without delving deep into complexities.

Diverse Model Creation: Keras endorses both Sequential and Functional APIs, catering to simple and complex neural architectures.

Ready Models: Keras boasts an array of pre-configured models, either for direct application or for adaptation to specific tasks.

Tailored Adjustments: Keras doesn't compromise on customization, allowing developers to define unique layers, optimization techniques, and more.

Relative Perspectives

Target & Specialty: While all three tools play pivotal roles in machine learning, their niches vary. TensorFlow shines in extensive neural networks, Scikit-learn excels in conventional machine learning endeavors, while Keras prioritizes user-friendly deep learning.

Depth vs. Accessibility: TensorFlow, being intricate, offers unparalleled depth but demands a sharper learning trajectory. Scikit-learn, with its intuitive design, appeals to newcomers. Keras manages to combine deep learning power with a user-centric design.

Community Backing: Each of these tools enjoys extensive community contributions, ensuring continuous refinements, feature enhancements, and a rich repository of resources for users.

Final Thoughts

The realm of machine learning offers diverse tools, each with its strengths. TensorFlow, Scikit-learn, and Keras have carved their niches, enabling researchers and practitioners to design effective solutions. The choice among them—or even their combined use—can pave the way for innovative, well-fitted solutions.

Cloud platforms in data science

Modern data science is deeply rooted in cloud technologies. As the world witnesses unparalleled data proliferation and soaring computational needs, conventional systems often become inadequate. Cloud infrastructures present themselves as an essential remedy, granting adaptive capabilities, synergized workspaces, and avant-garde tools designed for hefty data assignments. Here's an exploration of the intricate dance between cloud paradigms and the universe of data science.

The Rationale Behind the Affinity of Cloud in Data Science

Adaptable Computational Power: Traditional configurations come with fixed computational bandwidth. Cloud infrastructures, however, offer elasticity, modulating resources in tandem with workload needs, be it data assimilation, transformation, or algorithmic training.

Multi-faceted Storage Mechanisms: Contemporary data manifests in multiple avatars—orderly repositories, amorphous textual content, or dynamic data streams. Cloud solutions offer an array of storage blueprints, from object-oriented repositories to relational databases, ensuring each data form finds its fitting abode.

Cohesive Development Arenas: Teamwork lies at the heart of data science. Cloud avenues offer merged spaces where professionals can coherently ideate, refine, and usher models into reality, ensuring uniformity and trimming overlap.

Cutting-edge Analysis Instruments: Several cloud environments are equipped with ready-to-use analytical instruments, accelerating chores like data grooming, probing, or representation. This empowers data experts to channel their energies on unearthing revelations rather than tool orchestration.

Stalwarts of the Cloud Ecosystem

Amazon Web Services (AWS): Spearheading the cloud odyssey, AWS boasts an extensive arsenal primed for data science. While Amazon S3 stands as a formidable storage beacon, solutions like Amazon SageMaker simplify the labyrinth of machine learning. Concurrently, AWS's data lakes and diagnostic services blend data reshaping with introspection, offering a seamless data science trajectory.

Google Cloud Platform (GCP): GCP has etched its mark with its flair for artificial intelligence and machine learning. Beyond foundational computing and storage provisions, utilities like BigQuery propel expansive data introspection. Furthermore, AutoML, a signature tool, empowers stakeholders to sculpt machine-learning blueprints with scant coding.

Microsoft Azure: Azure's ethos aligns seamlessly with bridging cloud and data science. With a spotlight on AI-centric solutions, Azure's Machine Learning Studio provides a holistic milieu for algorithmic crafting and ushering. The platform also champions blended solutions, melding cloud advantages with terrestrial fortifications.

IBM Cloud: The fusion of IBM's cloud frontier with its mastery in data and AI yields a potent platform. Watson, the crown jewel of IBM's AI brigade, thrives in this cloud environment, offering suites from data spelunking to interactive AI. Complementing this are their cloud databases, architected for lightning-fast diagnostics.

Pioneering Shifts and Breakthroughs

Cloud environments aren't merely resource reservoirs; they're hubs of ingenuity. Reflect on the ascent of serverless paradigms: data scientists can orchestrate code reactions to triggers sans server oversight, refining fiscal and operational efficacy. There's also an evident tilt towards making machine learning accessible. Platforms are increasingly rolling out minimal-code solutions, enabling a broader spectrum of professionals to curate and deploy models.

Moreover, in an era where data governance is paramount, cloud realms are at the forefront of championing data sanctity and regulatory adherence. They're infusing tools to trace data origins, steward metadata, and chronicle data interactions, bolstering data's stature and reliability.

Fiscal Dynamics and Resource Optimization

Cloud domains address the fiscal contours of data science endeavors with finesse. Sidestepping hefty preliminary infrastructural outlays, the consumption-based billing model ensures entities only disburse for leveraged resources. Coupled with managed service structures, overheads tied to sustenance and evolution dwindle considerably.

Fortifying Security Landscapes

Relentless in their quest for robust defense mechanisms, cloud realms have escalated their protective measures. With provisions for data ciphering, in its dormant and transitory states, augmented authentication processes, and nuanced access stipulations, they ensure data's sanctum remains inviolable. Adherence to global compliance norms further augments this protective shield.

Epilogue

The synergistic liaison between cloud domains and data science is palpable. As the intricacies of data science burgeon, cloud infrastructures respond with agility, presenting not just avenues but also pioneering blueprints that navigate data science into uncharted territories. Amidst this harmonious interplay, decision-making processes stand to gain the most, as insights evolve to be more incisive, prompt, and operative.

Integration with AI platforms

The modern tech arena is significantly marked by the dominance of artificial intelligence (AI). Its self-directed algorithms and its adaptive capabilities have been integrated into a plethora of applications across varied sectors. The real essence of AI, however, gets magnified when seamlessly integrated with specialized platforms. This exploration endeavors to shed light on this synthesis, detailing its intricacies, benefits, and broader implications.

The Significance of this Fusion

AI models in isolation might often be confined, their potential limited by constraining environments. Distinctive platforms serve as expansive domains that provide AI models an environment for expansion, scalability, and ongoing enhancement.

Additionally, platforms introduce an organized architecture. They ensure a smooth journey from data collection to intricate analysis and from AI model training to its deployment, promising optimal performance.

Drivers of AI Integration

Several factors underscore this synthesis of AI with platforms:

Data Overflow: The digital footprint has seen explosive growth. Extracting meaningful knowledge from such vast data necessitates the amalgamation of AI's intelligence with strong platforms.

High Computational Requirements: Sophisticated AI models, especially those in deep learning, demand considerable computational strength. Platforms, equipped with distributed computational strategies and GPU enhancements, perfectly cater to these demands.

Instantaneous Analysis: Prompt decision-making is crucial in today's age. Platforms support quick data flows, enabling AI systems to immediately act upon incoming data streams.

Collaborative Endeavors: Today's AI solutions often require a collaborative effort. Platforms provide shared tools and a unified workspace, streamlining group-based AI projects.

Leading AI Platforms

Google's TensorFlow: Predominantly designed for deep learning, this open-source tool enables developers to create and educate intricate neural models. When integrated with TensorFlow Extended (TFX), its capabilities are enhanced, offering a complete solution for AI model deployment.

IBM Watson: Beyond being a standalone AI, when Watson is combined with IBM's cloud infrastructure, it transforms into a holistic toolset, ranging from data depiction to in-depth, AI-driven analytics.

Microsoft's Azure Machine Learning: As a cloud-supported platform, it's a treasure trove for AI enthusiasts. Its capabilities span from data processing to AI model deployment. Integration with tools like PowerBI emphasizes its analytical capabilities.

Amazon SageMaker: As a component of Amazon's robust AWS, SageMaker exemplifies the integration ethos, providing a comprehensive AI development setting.

Strategic Outcomes of the Integration

Enhanced Business Responsiveness: Enterprises can quickly adapt to market shifts. Integrated platforms ensure AI models are constantly updated, ensuring sharp and pertinent decision-making.

Tailored Solutions: These platforms are often modular, allowing firms to customize their AI approach, ensuring alignment with their unique demands.

Expandability: As enterprises expand, their analytical and data needs grow. Integrated systems inherently support growth, ensuring a seamless AI model expansion.

Security and Regulatory Adherence: Given AI's interaction with sensitive data, protection is crucial. Especially cloud-based AI platforms come fortified with top-tier security measures and often align with global regulations.

Emerging Trends

The AI and platform integration is a continuously evolving journey. Quantum computing is set to further elevate AI's computational prowess. Moreover, with the rise of edge computing, AI platforms will become more decentralized, driving AI analytics closer to the source.

Additionally, as the debate around AI ethics intensifies, platforms will adapt to include tools ensuring algorithmic neutrality, and championing responsible AI.

Concluding Thoughts

Integrating AI with specialized platforms is a tactical move, set to reshape both technology and commerce landscapes. As AI forges ahead, its synthesis with platforms ensures it does so with augmented capability, clear purpose, and a transformative vision across industries.

Chapter Fourteen

Case Studies in Data Science

Real-world applications

Today's rapidly evolving technological landscape seamlessly integrates with our everyday activities. This exploration highlights the transformative power of emerging disciplines such as artificial intelligence and data science, underscoring their role in reshaping industries, redefining societal dynamics, and enriching human existence.

Health Sector: Tailored Therapies and Proactive Health Insights

Advanced technologies are leaving an indelible mark on the healthcare domain. Through the lens of data analytics and smart algorithms, medical practitioners can anticipate health complications, craft individualized care approaches, and even foresee potential epidemic threats. Contemporary wearable gadgets harvest extensive data, fostering both individual insights and broader health implications. Furthermore, the advent of AI-empowered robotic surgeries promises unparalleled precision in specific contexts.

Transportation: The Era of Driverless Cars and Intelligent Traffic Systems

The vision of vehicles steering themselves is inching closer to fruition. Enhanced sensors, married to intelligent algorithms, empower cars to traverse intricate terrains with confidence. Beyond the cars themselves, digital tools are revolutionizing traffic management, predicting bottlenecks, and streamlining urban mobility.

Financial Realm: Smart Trading and Safeguarding Transactions

The fusion of technology in the financial arena has been transformative. High-speed trading bots interpret real-time market fluctuations, facilitating transactions at an unprecedented pace. Simultaneously, intelligent systems vigilantly monitor for anomalies, delivering instant fraud alerts and bolstering transactional security.

Agrarian Sector: High-Tech Farming and Crop Surveillance

Modern farmers are embracing technology-driven strategies. Aerial drones, equipped with sophisticated sensors, oversee crops, gauging their vitality and growth trajectory. Data-derived advisories assist farmers in watering, pest deterrence, and determining harvest periods, thus maximizing yield and resource efficacy.

Retail Landscape: Customized Retail Experiences and Efficient Stocking

The realm of shopping is undergoing a digital metamorphosis. Advanced algorithms decode consumer behavior, sculpting tailored product suggestions. In brick-and-mortar stores, IoT devices monitor stock levels, ensuring product availability and reducing overheads.

Entertainment Domain: Tailored Content and Immersive Experiences

Digital platforms utilize intricate algorithms to cater to content recommendations, heightening user engagement. Meanwhile, the domains of virtual and augmented reality usher in unparalleled experiences, spanning from gaming spectacles to digital exploration.

Energy Sector: Intelligent Energy Networks and Predictive Oversight

Energy consumption is evolving with the advent of smart grid systems. These networks, leverage data analytics, forecast demand, streamline resource distribution, and seamlessly incorporate renewable energy sources. Advanced tools pinpoint potential operational glitches in energy plants, ensuring consistent output.

Property Sphere: Automated Residences and Sustainable Urban Design

Innovative home systems, termed "smart homes", offer residents a novel dimension of environmental control. Concurrently, analytical tools are influencing city designs, fostering sustainable and accommodating urban centers for growing demographics.

Educational Arena: Customized Pedagogies and Borderless Learning

Digital learning platforms adapt content dynamically based on student interactions. Geographical boundaries dissolve with virtual learning spaces, fostering global discourse and knowledge exchange. Interactive tools, harnessing augmented reality, amplify learning engagement.

Environmental Sphere: Digital Conservation and Emission Monitoring

Tech-driven tools are pivotal in observing environmental shifts, from tracking animal patterns to gauging forest depletion. Such insights are invaluable for targeted conservation measures. Additionally, digital models forecast pollution trajectories, guiding timely countermeasures and policy decisions.

In Closing

The intricate tapestry of technological advances and their real-world manifestations presents a horizon brimming with potential. While certain challenges, like ethical quandaries and potential employment shifts, remain, the overarching benefits are palpable. As the digital age matures, its intertwining with our daily endeavors will only deepen, ushering us into an epoch characterized by heightened efficiency, comfort, and capabilities.

Success stories and lessons learned

Delving deep into the digital realm, countless businesses and pioneers have carved out remarkable victories. Each achievement, unique in its narrative, offers insights into strategic foresight, sheer tenacity, and at times, fortunate coincidences. However, the real treasure lies in the lessons these stories bring to the forefront, acting as catalysts for future innovations.

1. From Mail to Streaming: Netflix's Evolution

Netflix's journey, from dispatching DVDs via mail to being a global streaming titan, is a story of vision. Recognizing changing consumer habits and technological trends, they bravely transitioned into streaming and later, content creation.

Key Takeaway: Flexibility in business strategies is golden. In an ever-changing environment, adherence to outdated models can be detrimental. Being aware of and adapting to market dynamics is crucial.

2. The Advent of Digital Transactions: PayPal's Emergence

PayPal's rise to the zenith of digital payments is a tale of innovation. Identifying the inadequacies of conventional banking in the Internet age, they provided an effortless and protected online payment mechanism.

Key Takeaway: Pinpoint and address the inadequacies in prevailing systems. Conventional methods might fall short in newer contexts, presenting opportunities for innovative solutions.

3. Collaboration at Scale: Wikipedia's Success

The idea of an open, collaboratively constructed encyclopedia was audacious. However, Wikipedia surpassed expectations, showcasing the strength of collective knowledge-building.

Key Takeaway: Leveraging the collective expertise and cooperative nature of communities can be profoundly impactful. Platforms that tap into this potential can achieve unparalleled feats.

4. Transient Digital Connections: Snapchat's Innovation

In a digital era where traces are permanent, Snapchat brought in the concept of transitory content, differentiating itself amidst other social media platforms.

Key Takeaway: Offering a contrasting and unique user experience, even if it contradicts the norm, can set a brand apart.

5. The Art of Minimalism: Apple's Approach

Apple's offerings, from its pioneering computers to its smartphones, merged simplicity with sophistication. Their consistent commitment to design and functionality differentiated them.

Key Takeaway: A consistent emphasis on user-centric design can craft a distinct brand presence and cultivate a dedicated user base.

6. Powering Digital Stores: Shopify's Insight

Rather than rivaling e-commerce leaders, Shopify equipped individuals to establish their online stores, enabling countless to venture into e-commerce.

Key Takeaway: Empowering a broader audience, instead of competing head-on with industry leaders, can be a transformative strategy.

7. The Power of Open Source: Linux's Victory

While Linux wasn't a commercial entity, it posed an open-source alternative to commercial operating systems. Its legacy highlights the potential of projects driven by the community.

Key Takeaway: Financial success isn't restricted to closed systems. Community-driven, open initiatives can achieve significant influence.

8. Transforming Urban Transport: Uber's Breakthrough

Uber might not have been the originator of ride-sharing, but its strategic execution made it synonymous with the term. By addressing issues with traditional cab systems and leveraging the proliferation of smartphones, it reshaped urban transport.

Key Takeaway: Modern answers to traditional problems, especially when intertwined with tech advancements, can revolutionize sectors.

In summation, these narratives and their embedded lessons paint a rich mosaic of insights: adaptability, creativity, community collaboration, user-oriented approaches, and occasionally, the courage to rethink norms. As we journey through the tech epoch, these stories don't merely inspire but also guide our future endeavors.

The future scope of each application

Diving into the realms of emerging technologies, it's evident that every invention or system has a trajectory that projects beyond its current capabilities. As these technologies burgeon, their applications possess the power to transform sectors, reshape user interfaces, and pave the way for novel developments. Let's embark on an explorative journey into the prospective horizons of different technological applications.

1. Next-Gen Streaming Modalities:

Once a mere DVD rental service, Netflix has set the standard for worldwide digital content streaming. We could see it venturing into augmented and virtual realities for a more immersive user engagement. Also, AI's touch could lead to content tailoring, offering viewer-centric narrative experiences.

2. The Future of Digital Finances:

From its inception, PayPal has streamlined digital payments. Looking ahead, the integration of blockchain and decentralized finance models could redefine secure, transparent transactions. The dream of instant international transactions might soon be realized, obliterating existing time constraints.

3. Information Dissemination and Authentication:

Wikipedia's unique approach to information sharing might evolve to leverage sophisticated algorithms for data validation, ensuring reduced biases and inaccuracies. Envision an era where information absorption shifts from mere reading to interactive, experiential learning.

4. Advancing Fleeting Digital Engagements:

Snapchat's concept of momentary content captures contemporary data privacy sentiments. Future adaptations could see smarter content modulation, instantaneous AR integrations, and fortified algorithms to prioritize user privacy further.

5. Bridging Hardware Sophistication with Cognitive Abilities:

Apple's roadmap suggests a deeper infusion of AI, birthing devices that mimic human cognitive processes more closely. Visualize an era where our everyday experiences seamlessly blend digital and tangible realities.

6. E-commerce's Evolutionary Leap:

Shopify's democratization of e-commerce has been game-changing. Envision a world with global logistics at your fingertips, AI-curated market insights, and virtual reality-enhanced shopping escapades from home comforts.

7. The Surge of Transparent Tech Ecosystems:

Linux epitomizes the power of open source. As industries incline towards operational transparency, open-source might dominate fields as diverse as AI, quantum mechanics, and bio-innovations, fostering universal collaboration.

8. Green, Autonomous Urban Transit:

Uber's imprint on city transport is undeniable. Its future could be painted with green tech, self-driving vehicles, and broader urban logistical solutions, from aerial deliveries to ultra-speed transit partnerships.

9. Tailored Healthcare Solutions:

Tomorrow's healthcare might be characterized by AI for predictive diagnoses, augmented reality-aided surgeries, and real-time health telemetry through the Internet of Things. Wearable gadgets could proactively detect health deviations, and advanced telemedicine could redefine remote patient consultations.

10. Metropolis Meets Smart Tech:

Urban landscapes are on the cusp of a transformation into integrated smart systems. Intelligent algorithms could optimize traffic, sanitation, power consumption, and public safety, weaving an urban tapestry of efficiency.

11. Future-Proofing Agriculture:

The agricultural sector is ripe for tech interventions. Imagine drones monitoring vast farmlands, AI identifying and combating pests, and smart irrigation adapting to real-time weather conditions.

12. Gaming's Quantum Leap:

Gaming's horizon hints at VR-driven worlds, AI-responsive storylines, and quantum-fueled multiplayer universes that blur the lines between game and reality.

In conclusion, the frontier of potential technological applications is vast and pulsating with possibilities. As the digital age accelerates, established norms will be challenged, birthing hybrid solutions that enhance and perhaps even transcend human experiences. As we sail these exciting waters, adaptability and perpetual upskilling will be our trusted compasses.

Chapter Fifteen

Building a Career in Data Science

Roles and responsibilities in the data science domain

In today's data-driven landscape, the domain of data science interweaves a combination of statistical, computational, and domain-specific expertise to unveil insights from vast arrays of data. As the field garners more attention, a plethora of specialized roles have surfaced. Let's navigate through these roles to understand the nuances and expectations attached to each.

1. Data Scientist:

This central figure in the data science universe has a wide purview:

- Crafting relevant questions that align with business goals.

- Orchestrating intricate analytical experiments.

- Deciphering and relaying findings.

- Harnessing machine learning and advanced techniques for predictive analytics.

2. Data Analyst:

These professionals dig deep into data:

- Preparing, refining, and representing data.

- Deriving concrete recommendations from datasets.

- Keeping a tab on critical metrics.

- Conducting rigorous tests to guide business strategies.

3. Data Engineer:

These are the builders of data infrastructures:

- Crafting, managing, and upkeeping robust data pipelines.

- Merging varied data sources into unified systems.

- Ensuring data is primed for analytical pursuits.

- Partnering with data scientists to make machine learning models a reality.

4. Machine Learning Engineer:

Beyond generic data analytics, they specialize in:

- Sculpting algorithms rooted in statistical models.

- Refining and adapting machine learning methods.

- Transitioning models from development to deployment.

- Engaging with data scientists to mold models into functional software.

5. Statistician:

The mathematical pillars of the data domain:

- Leveraging statistical theories for tangible challenges.

- Employing specialized software for data evaluation.

- Translating statistical outcomes into actionable insights.

- Counseling on the strengths and constraints of statistical techniques.

6. Data and Analytics Manager:

Orchestrating the entire data team:

- Supervising the lifecycle of data-centric projects.

- Aligning analytical initiatives with overarching business aspirations.

- Synchronizing various departments for cohesive data strategies.

- Reflecting on data project results to drive future endeavors.

7. Business Intelligence (BI) Developer:

With a keen focus on business implications:

- Architecting strategies to expedite information access for business decisions.

- Utilizing platforms such as Tableau and Power BI for visual interpretations.

- Aligning closely with stakeholders to tailor systems to business needs.

8. Data Visualization Specialist:

Masters of translating data into visuals:

- Crafting graphical interpretations of data narratives.

- Harnessing tools like Seaborn, D3.js, and more.

- Engaging with data-focused roles to paint the broader picture.

9. Database Administrator:

Guarding and overseeing the data repositories:

- Ensuring consistent, secure, and uninterrupted database access.

- Overseeing database security measures.

- Executing database backups and restoration processes.

10. Big Data Expert:

Navigating the vast oceans of data:

- Handling expansive datasets via platforms such as Spark and Hadoop.

- Partnering with data professionals for scalable solutions.

- Tackling challenges tied to real-time data management.

In summation, while each role in the data science ecosystem has its distinctive scope, collaboration threads them together. The narratives crafted by Data Visualization Specialists gain depth from the insights of Data Scientists, all underpinned by the infrastructure established by Data Engineers. In this realm, individual expertise amalgamates to shape the compelling symphony of data-driven strategies and solutions.

Required skill sets and how to acquire them

In the rapidly evolving landscape of data science, possessing the right amalgamation of skills can be a game-changer for one's career trajectory and the fruition of data projects. Identifying these pivotal abilities and mapping out strategies to cultivate them is essential. Let's explore the essential skills in data science and understand how to effectively cultivate them.

1. Coding Expertise:

Essence: Formulating algorithms, tweaking data, and establishing models necessitate a foundational grasp of programming.

Development Path: Delve into languages like Python or R through online platforms such as Codecademy or edX. Regular coding challenges on platforms like HackerEarth or Codewars can hone this skill.

2. Adeptness in Statistical Reasoning:

Essence: Extracting value from data requires a grasp of statistical methodologies and probabilistic theories.

Development Path: Consider structured coursework in statistics or modules from platforms like StatQuest or Coursera. Applying these concepts in data challenges on platforms like Kaggle can solidify understanding.

3. Understanding of Machine Learning Paradigms:

Essence: Building predictive models and sophisticated analytics relies on machine learning know-how.

Development Path: Engage with in-depth resources from institutions like MIT OpenCourseWare or Fast.ai, emphasizing algorithm fundamentals. Practicing through side projects or contributing to community-led initiatives can fortify comprehension.

4. Database Savviness:

Essence: The essence of data management lies in the proficient handling of databases and storage solutions.

Development Path: Interactive tutorials from platforms like Dataquest or Codecademy focusing on SQL can be invaluable. Venturing into NoSQL databases through hands-on projects can also provide a broader perspective.

5. Data Preparation Proficiency:

Essence: Addressing inconsistencies in raw data and making it actionable is paramount.

Development Path: Engage with resources such as Towards Data Science articles spotlighting libraries like Pandas. Directly working with diverse datasets can provide a tangible understanding of common issues.

6. Visualization Capabilities:

Essence: Crafting compelling visual narratives from data aids in impactful communication.

Development Path: Explore resources like Data Visualization Society or online tutorials on tools like Seaborn. Recreating and analyzing visual stories from varied sources can foster a deeper appreciation.

7. Familiarity with Big Data Solutions:

Essence: Processing extensive datasets mandates the adoption of platforms like Spark or Hadoop.

Development Path: Deep-dive courses from sources like Big Data University or Cloudera offer specialized insights. Setting up personal big data environments or experimenting in sandbox modes can be enlightening.

8. Interpersonal Skills and Business Insight:

Essence: Alongside technical capabilities, grasping business objectives and communicating solutions effectively is pivotal.

Development Path: Workshops emphasizing effective collaboration or business-oriented courses on platforms like Harvard Business Review can be instrumental. Direct interaction in business environments, even beyond data realms, can be invaluable.

9. Commitment to Ongoing Learning:

Essence: With the relentless pace of technological advancement, staying updated is non-negotiable.

Development Path: Active engagement in seminars, symposiums, or tech meetups can be beneficial. Regularly reading industry-focused publications or blogs like Medium's data science section ensures a steady flow of contemporary insights.

10. Specialized Domain Knowledge:

Essence: Given the wide-ranging applications of data science, industry-specific acumen can significantly enhance outcomes.

Development Path: Depending on the target sector (e.g., automotive, pharmaceuticals), consider domain-focused training or credentials. Networking with industry experts can also offer invaluable perspectives.

In conclusion, acquiring core data science competencies is a multifaceted endeavor, intertwining formal education, hands-on experience, and an innate thirst for knowledge. As one embarks on this skill-enhancement journey, a mix of structured learning and pragmatic application emerges as the cornerstone for achieving excellence in this dynamic field. Whether one is starting out or is an established data science practitioner, a methodical and engaged approach to skill enhancement can open doors to unparalleled achievements.

Future trends in data science jobs

As technological growth intersects with the surge of data, the significance of data science in business and innovation has become paramount. As more sectors recognize the benefits of interpreting vast amounts of data, there's a growing demand for experts in the domain. This ever-evolving sector is bound to undergo several shifts in the coming years. Let's delve into the upcoming trends that will potentially redefine careers in data science.

1. Specialization Becomes the Norm:

Gone are the days when "data scientist" was a blanket term. The future points towards more specialized roles, from experts in machine learning applications to those adept at crafting impactful data visualizations. This move towards specialization promotes depth of expertise and encourages diverse collaboration.

2. Blending of Industry Knowledge with Data Expertise:

Specialized sectors such as healthcare or finance require a tailored approach to data interpretation. We might soon see titles like "Healthcare Data Analyst" or "Financial Data Strategist." This combination of industry-specific expertise with data analytical skills will lead to more relevant and actionable insights.

3. The Rise of AutoML:

While tools designed to automate various machine learning tasks are becoming popular, they don't necessarily diminish the need for human data scientists. AutoML tackles repetitive tasks, leaving data professionals free to address more complex and strategic challenges.

4. Advanced Data Management Techniques:

With the data deluge, manual data processing is increasingly challenging. Enhanced data management, using AI and ML, will simplify processes like data cleaning and enrichment. This means data scientists can allocate more time to data analysis rather than preliminary tasks.

5. Prioritizing Ethical Data Use:

The increasing influence of algorithms in decision-making brings along concerns about transparency, bias, and fairness. Data professionals will play a crucial role in ensuring ethical considerations in AI applications, blending technical skills with societal and ethical understanding.

6. Intersection of Quantum Computing and Data:

Quantum computing, with its superior processing power, can revolutionize data analysis. As it evolves, there will be a growing need for data experts familiar with quantum methodologies.

7. Constant Evolution and Learning:

Given the rapid advancements in the field, data professionals must be dedicated to perpetual learning, whether through formal education, online courses, or staying updated with recent research.

8. Emphasis on Interpersonal Skills:

Beyond technical acumen, future data scientists must be adept communicators and collaborators. Explaining complex data findings in digestible terms will be a sought-after skill, leading to roles that value both technical and interpersonal strengths.

9. Emergence of Data Liaisons:

The role of "data liaison" or "data translator" is becoming more crucial. These individuals bridge the technical and business domains, ensuring insights are both actionable and aligned with business objectives.

10. Global and Flexible Work Dynamics:

Recent global events have propelled the acceptance of remote working. Data science, which naturally fits this model, will continue to lean towards distributed teams, allowing companies to source talent globally and offer professionals a flexible work environment.

In conclusion, the horizon of data science careers is expansive, marked by both niche expertise and the need for broader skill sets. As businesses strive to harness data in innovative ways, the experts they employ will need to adapt continually. With a blend of deep technical knowledge and a broad understanding of business and ethics, data professionals are set to be cornerstone assets in the future's data-centric landscape.

Conclusions

Recap of the book's journey

Drawing towards the end of this literary expedition, it's pivotal to look back and appreciate the vast array of topics, insights, and understandings that have been shared. This summary aims to provide a succinct reflection on the diverse themes that have colored our pages and enlightened our discussions.

The book embarked on foundational discussions, painting the backdrop of our subject. From the nascent stages to its contemporary nuances, the evolution was meticulously tracked. This exploration offered a comprehensive understanding of the genesis and subsequent trajectory of the domain.

As we progressed, intricate mechanics took center stage. Detailed methodologies, profound debates, and critical appraisals enriched our journey. Through vivid illustrations and compelling data, theoretical nuances were transformed into relatable insights, ensuring an immersive experience for the reader.

Our voyage was further augmented by the contributions from industry stalwarts. Their firsthand experiences and seasoned perspectives offered a bridge between academic discourse and real-world applications, infusing the narrative with depth and authenticity.

Of particular note were segments addressing widespread myths and potential roadblocks. These sections, by confronting misconceptions and underlining challenges, offered a well-rounded view of the terrain, arming readers with the knowledge to navigate with both enthusiasm and prudence.

A defining feature was the interactive elements sprinkled throughout. These tools, ranging from quizzes to reflective exercises, encouraged active engagement, transforming readers into active participants in their learning journey.

Subsequent chapters heralded a thematic evolution. From core concepts, the focus shifted to real-world applications, dissecting the influence of our subject across multiple industries and paradigms. The interplay between theoretical constructs and practical realities was vividly depicted, broadening our understanding.

The latter portions of the book ventured into the realms of ethics and philosophy. More than just technical discourses, these chapters probed the deeper societal and human implications of our discussions, spurring readers to deliberate on larger questions of morality and impact.

As we neared the end, a treasure trove of further resources was shared. Lists of extended readings, reference materials, and avenues for deeper research ensured the book's role as a catalyst for continued intellectual pursuit.

In retrospect, this literary endeavor has been comprehensive and enlightening, spanning from the rudiments to the avant-garde. Through its pages, a holistic understanding has been fostered, instilling both knowledge and an appetite for continued discovery.

In summation, this book stands as a guiding light for those venturing into this domain. Its blend of academic rigor and practical insights ensures a well-rounded perspective. As we conclude our journey, the hope remains that the insights gained will kindle further curiosity and drive an enduring zeal for exploration.

The future of data science

As we stand at the cusp of a new era, the evolution of data science emerges as a focal point in the world of technology. From its modest beginnings as a realm of statistical evaluations, it has now blossomed into a behemoth, marrying complex algorithms with expansive data pools. Looking ahead, we can forecast several pivotal shifts that will shape the trajectory of this dynamic discipline.

A significant revolution in sight is the anticipated rise in the realm of automation. The concept of Machine Learning Operations (MLOps) is set to redefine many stages of the data workflow, spanning from data curation to the deployment of models. This shift aims to streamline operations, granting data experts the bandwidth to grapple with more complex challenges and diminishing the burden of routine tasks.

On the frontier of technological innovation, quantum computing beckons with potential that could recalibrate our understanding of data processing. As it unfolds, quantum mechanisms could outshine conventional binary systems, bringing forth an era where data computations occur at unimaginable scales and velocities. Such advancements could radically transform data analytics, intricate simulations, and instantaneous data processing.

Furthermore, the impending fusion of data science with emerging technologies presages a future rich in collaborative progress. Envision a world where data analytics meets the secure world of blockchain, offering unmatched levels of transactional integrity. Or, imagine a symbiosis between data visualization and augmented reality (AR), reimagining how data is perceived and interacted with.

In terms of industry-specific advancements, healthcare presents a fertile ground for data-driven transformations. The convergence of genomics with data analytics can give rise to tailored medical treatments, allowing for therapies aligned with individual genetic profiles, leading to enhanced efficacy and minimizing adverse effects. Wearable technologies, paired with analytical foresight, might provide real-time health insights, fostering a paradigm shift from reactive care to proactive health management.

In the financial and commercial spheres, data science's influence is set to burgeon further. Advanced analytical models could soon inform investment decision-making, risk evaluation, and security protocols. In retail, a merger between real-time analytics and the Internet of Things (IoT) can usher in the age of intelligent storefronts, where every aspect, from stock control to consumer behavior, is refined using data-derived insights.

However, this luminous horizon isn't without its clouds. The increasing prowess of data science brings to the fore pressing ethical dilemmas related to data usage, protection, and inclusivity. As the boundaries of what's possible expand, a global emphasis on ethical harnessing of data becomes paramount. Ensuring individual privacy, fair access to benefits, and preventing potential misapplications will be at the heart of the conversation.

Simultaneously, the expanding horizon of data science amplifies the urgency to bridge the impending skills rift. With the discipline's multifaceted nature, a gap between existing skills and evolving industry needs is inevitable. Collaborative ventures between educational institutions and industry, coupled with an emphasis on perpetual learning, will be instrumental in navigating this challenge.

In conclusion, data science's future, resplendent with opportunities, also beckons with nuanced complexities. The ensuing chapter promises rapid innovations, holistic integrations, and industry-specific metamorphoses. However, as we journey forward, the compass that guides should be one of responsible innovation, ensuring that technological progress is always tethered to ethical considerations.

Encouraging continuous learning

In today's swiftly changing technological environment, the classic model of fixed education struggles to keep pace. As the relentless progression of technology continues, particularly in areas deeply rooted in innovation, there's an ever-increasing emphasis on championing an enduring learning mentality.

Continuous learning is the deliberate, ongoing effort to expand one's knowledge, both for personal growth and professional advancement. Unlike traditional educational trajectories with a clear start and finish, continuous learning is an infinite journey. It recognizes the fact that the realm of human understanding is ever-evolving, necessitating individuals to remain adaptable.

Here are the primary reasons underscoring this learning paradigm's importance:

Rapid Technological Shifts: The current tech-driven era is marked by breakthroughs such as AI, quantum computing, and in-depth data processing. Being in their formative phases, frequent shifts and updates emerge. Past knowledge can quickly become obsolete, emphasizing the need for recurrent updating.

Evolving Job Profiles: Today's professional landscape, especially in fields like IT, finance, and data analytics, has roles that were previously unheard of. As these roles transform, continuous skill enhancement becomes paramount.

Worldwide Integration: We're now more connected globally than ever before. This increased integration results in a melting pot of varied cultures and ideas. Continuous learning facilitates a deeper understanding of these global nuances, ensuring effective collaboration.

So, how can one promote an ethos of continuous learning, both individually and organizationally?

Embedding Learning Mechanisms: Firms can integrate learning into their daily operations. Regular training sessions, access to digital learning resources, or setting aside dedicated self-learning periods can be effective. Some leading companies, like Google, even set aside time for employees to engage in personal projects, encouraging innovative thinking and learning.

Utilizing Digital Platforms: The Internet offers an array of resources tailored to diverse learning preferences. Platforms like Coursera or Udacity provide specialized courses, while communities like Stack Overflow or ResearchGate facilitate peer-to-peer knowledge exchange.

Fostering an Inquisitive Mindset: On a personal level, it's essential to cultivate an innate sense of wonder. Shifting one's perspective of learning from a task to a journey can make the experience more fulfilling.

Community Engagement: Collective learning can often provide more profound insights than solitary study. Engaging in learning communities or professional networks can expose individuals to varied viewpoints and challenge their existing beliefs.

Iterative Feedback: Continuous improvement requires consistent feedback. Regular evaluations, understanding what techniques are effective, and refining one's approach are crucial. For example, if visual learning isn't effective, exploring podcasts might be more suitable.

In essence, in this dynamic age, the concept of "Survival of the fittest" has evolved. Today, 'fitness' pertains to one's cognitive flexibility, skill versatility, and an unending quest for knowledge. Championing continuous learning is not just an aspirational aim but a fundamental necessity for both individuals and institutions to thrive in the modern world.

www.ingramcontent.com/pod-product-compliance
Lightning Source LLC
LaVergne TN
LVHW051338050326
832903LV00031B/3606